PAID TO SPEAK

PAID TO SPEAK

Best Practices for Building a Successful Speaking Business

NATIONAL SPEAKERS ASSOCIATION

GREENLEAF
BOOK GROUP PRESS

Published by Greenleaf Book Group Press
Austin, Texas
www.gbgpress.com

Copyright ©2011 National Speakers Association

Distributed by Greenleaf Book Group LLC

For ordering information or special discounts for bulk purchases, please contact Greenleaf Book Group LLC at PO Box 91869, Austin, TX 78709, 512.891.6100.

Design and composition by Greenleaf Book Group LLC and Alex Head
Cover design by Greenleaf Book Group LLC and Dan Pitts

Cataloging-in-Publication data

Paid to speak : best practices for building a successful speaking business /
    [edited by] National Speakers Association. — 1st ed.

    p. ; cm.

  ISBN: 978-1-60832-131-5

  1. Public speaking—Vocational guidance. 2. Success in business. I.
National Speakers Association (U.S.)

PN4098   .P25 2011
808.5/1/023

Part of the Tree Neutral® program, which offsets the number of trees consumed in the production and printing of this book by taking proactive steps, such as planting trees in direct proportion to the number of trees used: www.treeneutral.com

TreeNeutral®

Printed in the United States of America on acid-free paper

11 12 13 14 15 16   10 9 8 7 6 5 4 3 2 1

First Edition

CONTENTS

Acknowledgments ix

Introduction: Charting Your Professional Growth: Using NSA's
Professional Competencies 1
Jim Cathcart, CSP, CPAE

Eloquence

Chapter 1: The Elements of Eloquence 9
Glenna Salsbury, CSP, CPAE

Chapter 2: What's Your Story? 15
Sam Horn

Chapter 3: The Impact of Stories 21
Max W. Dixon

Chapter 4: When Presenting Becomes Facilitating 29
Kristin Arnold, MBA, CFP, CMC, CSP

Chapter 5: Facilitation 101: The Six Roles of Effective Facilitators 39
Jonathan Tessier

Chapter 6: A Pause Can Build Applause 45
Lou Heckler, CSP, CPAE

Chapter 7: Improv Rules! Five Ways to Make Your Speeches More Powerful
and Engaging 49
Gilda Bonanno

Chapter 8: Cooking Up Comedy. 57
Molly Cox, Dale Irvin CSP, CPAE, Bill Stainton, and Ron Culberson, MSW, CSP

Chapter 9: Move Your Audience with the Right Body Language 67
Patti Wood, MA, CSP

Chapter 10: Dress for Success 77
Janice Hurley-Trailor

Chapter 11: From Backstage to Onstage: Prepare to Shine!................... 85
Kevin E. O'Connor, CSP, and Cyndi Maxey, CSP

Enterprise

Chapter 12: Top Ten Biggest Challenges Professional Speakers Face Today....... 93
Nido R. Qubein, CSP, CPAE

Chapter 13: Seven Keys to Get Up, Get Speaking, and Get Paid 101
David Newman

Chapter 14: Simply the Best! Create a Compelling and Authentic Brand for
Your Speaking Enterprise 109
Dick Bruso

Chapter 15: Monetize Your Message: Turn Your Presentations into
Additional Income... 115
Kim Clausen

Chapter 16: Power Partnerships: Working with Bureaus.................... 121
Holli Catchpole

Chapter 17: How to Spice Up Your Writing 127
Dianna Booher, MA, CSP, CPAE

Chapter 18: Land that Book Contract! 137
Rich Gallagher

Chapter 19: Use Verbal Ping-Pong to Get a Rise from Your Elevator Speech...... 145
Brian Walter, CSP

Chapter 20: Your Name in Lights! How to Capitalize on the Power of Publicity.... 153
Pam Lontos, MA, CSP

Expertise

Chapter 21: A Niche Can Make You Rich............................... 165
LeAnn Thieman, CSP, CPAE

Chapter 22: Tell the Right Story at the Right Time 173
Bruce Hale

Chapter 23: How to Write a Compelling Book Proposal.................... 181
Barbara Glanz, CSP

Chapter 24: Seven Strategies to Guide You Through the Virtual World 189
Susan Friedmann, CSP, and Gina Schreck, CSP

Chapter 25: Four Big Reasons Why Speakers Should Blog 197
Jeff Korhan

Chapter 26: The Ins and Outs of Licensing. 203
Jim Hennig, PhD, CSP, CPAE

Ethics

Chapter 27: Ethics: The Hot New "E" Word 211
Rita Barreto Craig

Chapter 28: Walk Your Own Talk 217
Al Walker, CSP, CPAE

Chapter 29: Setting a Code of Professional Ethics for the Speaking Profession . . . 223
Stacy Tetschner, CAE

Why Should You Join a Professional Association? 227

ACKNOWLEDGMENTS

This book is the result of the combined efforts of individuals who were willing to share their expertise with the National Speakers Association (NSA). In addition to the authors who contributed their rich content knowledge, NSA also acknowledges the following individuals for their roles in the completion of this book:

Content Advisors/Reviewers
Francis Bologna, CPA
Frank Bucaro, CSP, CPAE
Mike Faber
Shirley Garrett, CSP, EdD
Eliz Greene
Martin Grunder
Louis Heckler, CSP, CPAE
Sam Horn
Max Jaffe, CPA
Michael McKinley, CSP, CPAE
Deborah Merriman
John B. Molidor, PhD
David Newman
Beth M. Ramsay
Gary Rifkin
Stephen Schumann
Marilynn Semonick, CSP
Linda Swindling, CSP, JD

Design, Marketing, and Publishing
Greenleaf Book Group, LLC

Editors
Stephanie R. Conner
Barbara Parus
Jake Poinier

Project Leaders
Barbara Parus
Mandy Schulze
Stacy Tetschner, CAE

INTRODUCTION

CHARTING YOUR PROFESSIONAL GROWTH: USING NSA'S PROFESSIONAL COMPETENCIES

Jim Cathcart, CSP, CPAE

One of the great tragedies in the speaking business is when someone becomes exceptional in one or two areas of competence, but hits a slump or fails because other competencies have been neglected.

One speaker might be great at selling and generating lots of bookings, for example, but never get repeat sales due to poor performance. For another, the reverse could happen: great performances that yield no bookings because of a poor professional reputation or lousy business management. Some speakers burn out from too much speaking and not enough development of products to carry the message and generate revenue when the speaker is at rest—what I call SWISS money: Sales While I Sleep Soundly. And then there's the exceptional communicator who speaks brilliantly until there's a glitch with the sound or lighting, or the speaker who has great natural ability that goes undeveloped for lack of investing time in topic research.

Speakers need to take time each year to stop and assess their professional growth. After all, that's what will determine results a year from now and beyond. I find it helpful to have a tool to stimulate my thinking and expand my awareness. The following Wheel of Professional Competency helps examine the balance between each of the eight key areas of professional growth that were adopted by the National Speakers Association in 1985 as the backbone of professional development. The current format is called the Four E's: Eloquence, Expertise, Ethics, and Enterprise; each of the four includes two of the competencies.

Here is how to use it: First, read the balance of this article to get a refresher on the exact definition of each competency. Next, think about what you consider to be "beginner," "master," etc., in each category. Then, plot your current status on each of the lines. For example, if you are unaware of the inner workings of NSA and all of its offerings, or you haven't stayed on top of happenings and developments in the meetings industry, then your rating in Professional Awareness would be somewhere between a one (beginner) and a six (experienced)—even if you have twenty years in the business. If you haven't kept up in this area, then your *current* professional awareness is relatively low.

Next, do a similar assessment of yourself in each of the seven other competencies. There will probably be a wide variation in your ratings from one competency to the next. And there may be variation in each individual competency from one year to the next. All of them are in constant motion as a speaker grows.

After assessing all eight areas, step back and look at your wheel. Notice the

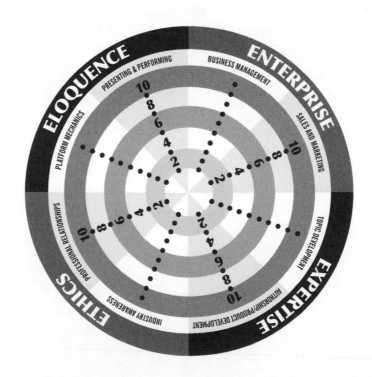

variations in your ratings from one line to the next. Now, connect the ratings on each line to the ones around it with your pencil.

The shape created by these lines reflects where you need to focus your energies for growth. In some areas, you may be operating at the master level, while in others you may be just experienced or even beginner. The ratings change from time to time based on the attention paid to growing each area.

The Wheel of Professional Competency is a handy way to check yourself and see how things are progressing or receding. Date each iteration of your chart, and watch its evolution over the years. Patterns will emerge that not only keep your growth on track and well balanced, but also teach you other things about yourself.

To bolster skills in a particular area, consult the NSA offerings in that competency. A complete listing of tapes, labs and workshops, articles, and special presentations, identified by competency, is available from NSA headquarters. Visit www.NSAspeaker.org to mix and match your education to meet your current and anticipated needs.

A QUARTER CENTURY OF COMPETENCY

In 1985, the professional development program of NSA was organized around the major areas of professional competence needed by all speakers, regardless of their primary topic, unique style or area of specialty. The Eight Professional Competencies encompass all of the skills and knowledge needed for optimum professional performance, regardless of what type of speaker you are.

Special consideration has been given to the unique needs of each individual and the great diversity among speakers. A master list of 50 primary topics was developed to guide the people who plan NSA meetings and publications in selecting a balanced program of information that will serve fairly the needs of all members of our profession.

While the 50 topics were intended to be updated from time to time—based on changes in the global economy, technology, and business community—the Eight Professional Competencies were not. *The Eight Professional Competencies are the basic categories of skill, knowledge, or mastery needed by all who speak professionally.* These competencies allow for endless variations in specific content and focus based upon the choices of the individual and the needs of the moment.

It was originally intended that these competencies would become the guide by which NSA's leaders could measure whether programs and publications were meeting the needs of all of its members—avoiding too much emphasis on one area, such as sales and marketing, or too little on other areas such as business management. Since, on some level, all eight competencies are needed by all speakers, the resources of NSA could be balanced among the eight.

These competencies are also the backbone of the Certified Speaking Professional (CSP) certification process. "Professionalism" among speakers can only be certified by combining a balanced, thorough professional education with significant actual experience gained in the speaking profession, while adhering to an established set of standards for professional conduct.

DEFINING THE EIGHT COMPETENCIES

The *Eloquence* Competencies

1. **Platform Mechanics: Knowing and mastering all of the "mechanical" skills of performing as a speaker.** These include:

    Staging, lighting, choreography (movement), and sound systems that apply to each type of speaking. What they are, how they work, and how to best use them for the desired effect.

    Performing on video, audio, online, or via satellite versus face-to-face. Strategies for dealing with the most common speaking problems; for example, distractions, emergencies, inoperable equipment, poor lighting, temperature extremes, time constraints, etc.

    Group dynamics and crowd control techniques. Differences in delivery style required to reach small versus large groups, generate or stop group involvement, increase or decrease drama, etc.

2. **Presenting & Performing: Knowing how to reach your audience in the manner that will achieve your desired effect.** Includes:

    Knowing how to develop and deliver stories, the use of humor, voice control, ways to tailor your message to an audience, and the latest concepts in communication. Understanding psychology and adult learning theory.

    Acting skills for speakers, how to be a master of ceremonies or lead a panel, how to create and lead a seminar or workshop, etc. Keynote versus concurrent session techniques.

The *Enterprise* Competencies

3. **Business Management: Knowing how to deal with the administrative side of the speaking business; contracts, agreements, systems, and money.** Includes:

   Contracts, agreements, royalties, and fees. Hiring and managing staff and resource personnel. Dealing with suppliers. Travel strategies. Managing your money. Licenses, taxes, and visas.

   Understanding office technology, systems, and equipment. Inventory control and records management. Scheduling, confirming, and tracking engagements. Client files, speech note files, and how to handle the paperwork appropriately.

4. **Sales and Marketing: Knowing how to generate engagements and expand your impact within your chosen markets.** Includes:

   How to penetrate a market or account, selling to associations vs. corporations, various sales techniques (phone, mail, expositions, in person, etc.), designing brochures and promotional materials.

   Selling speeches, seminars, individual enrollments, rallies, products, and selling your writing. How to create a celebrity image in your chosen markets.

The *Expertise* Competencies

5. **Topic Development: Knowing how to select and expand the topics which are of greatest value to you.** Includes:

   Selecting the right topic for your goals, interests, and skills. Identifying the topics most appropriate for your audience. Research techniques for expanding your materials and knowledge. How to use research assistants and gain access to other resources. How to become an expert on your topic.

   Finding and developing materials to supplement your speech. Roll-out techniques, such as expanding your speech into a seminar, or an article into a workbook, book, audio script, or video performance.

6. **Authorship/Product Development: Knowing how to convert your speaking message into other forms in order to reach more or different audiences.** Includes:

Writing techniques, understanding and dealing with the publishing community (editors, agents, and publishers), knowing the mechanics and strategies of developing various types of products. Recognizing the strengths and limitations of each medium.

How to write and produce a book, audio, video, learning library, article, series of products, etc. Understanding printing, binding, video taping, and publishing to the extent relevant for your needs.

The *Ethics* Competencies

7. **Professional Awareness: Knowing the state of the art in speaking and understanding our industry or profession.** Includes:

Understanding NSA; how it works, what it does, where it stands in the profession and among those who speak professionally.

Understanding the meetings and conventions industry; who the players are, what the issues are, what is going on, and how it affects speakers.

Understanding domestic and world affairs as they affect speakers, and keeping abreast of the latest developments in the speaking field.

8. **Professional Relationships: Knowing the interests, needs and issues in dealing with our clients, colleagues, suppliers, and coworkers in the speaking profession.**

Understanding the meeting planner, speakers bureaus and agents, our fellow speakers, and those who serve the meetings industry. Knowing the latest concerns and developments relating to any of the above.

Jim Cathcart, CSP, CPAE, 1988-1989 NSA president and Cavett Award recipient in 1993, is the creator of the eight competencies used by NSA since 1985. He has been a full-time speaker since 1977.

THE ELEMENTS OF ELOQUENCE

Glenna Salsbury, CSP, CPAE

Eloquence. We know it when we see it—or when we hear and feel it. But defining eloquence may be a different endeavor. Pascal said, "Eloquence is a painting of the thoughts." Webster's dictionary defines it as "the fluent, skillful use of words to persuade or move hearers or readers."

Those definitions certainly capture a speaker's goal. The question remains: How does one achieve eloquence on the platform? What are the essential ingredients that produce a powerful, eloquent presentation?

Perhaps we must first agree that the audience intuitively recognizes eloquence. Hence, the essence of eloquence may be best explored from the listener's viewpoint.

There are five elements that come together to create eloquence.

ELEMENT #1: THE ATMOSPHERE

Create an atmosphere of friendship and intimacy. This task is the presenter's responsibility.

The room setup is critical in creating a friendly environment. Ideally there should be no empty seats. If the room is arranged theater-style, be sure there are fewer chairs than anticipated attendees. Stacked chairs nearby can be kept for any overflow. If the seats are stationary, as in an auditorium, then rope off the back of the room. Room setup is an essential part of coordinating with the meeting planner. For example, the event may be a dinner with round tables. It is important to request that the tables be placed as close to the presentation stage as possible and as close to one another as possible.

Finally, it is critical for you as the presenter to arrive early enough to verify the room arrangement. If changes need to be made, they need to be handled in cooperation with the meeting planner. Speakers should not direct the venue's staff to make the changes.

You may be wondering *why* the seating issue is so critical. The answer? The *energy* is lessened or even lost entirely wherever there is "dead" space in a room. Energy is sustained and even increased when people are shoulder to shoulder—warmth and friendship are enhanced by physical closeness. This is also why center aisles are not ideal. A speaker's energy dissipates when he or she speaks into that empty aisle.

Meet and greet participants personally as they arrive.

When feasible, a speaker should request that attendees have nametags, with the first name especially large and readable.

Then, as people enter the room, greet them warmly. Ask meaningful questions that relate to the presentation. For example, if the theme or objective of the meeting is enhancing customer service, a good question might be, "What is the biggest challenge you face in meeting customers' expectations?"

During your presentation, honor those you have met by referencing their wisdom or answering their questions.

Practice self-revelation, even self-deprecation, as you begin your program.

An audience wants to know you are authentic and genuinely present with them.

One of the best ways to demonstrate this is to poke fun at yourself early in your presentation. If you have a habit of speaking rapidly, for example, set up a humorous disclaimer. Or you may have an obvious challenge, like a broken leg, for example. Make fun out of what may be a potential distraction.

Remember, other than food and shelter, human beings' greatest needs are love and appreciation. By tuning in to your listeners you honor them. And by creating a sense of intimacy in the physical room arrangement, you will enhance the camaraderie from the outset.

ELEMENT #2: THE SPEAKER'S COMFORT

Create a climate of comfort for yourself.

When the speaker is nervous, tentative, or uncomfortable in any way, the audience senses this. There is an invisible, yet very distracting, tension that prevails.

Presenters need to create a relaxed, secure environment for themselves on the platform. When you are at peace, comfortable, and free from personal preoccupations or concerns, the energy in the room becomes relaxed and free.

The stage setup is critical in determining your comfort level. Ideally, you and the meeting planner have agreed upon your needs and preferences. Typical considerations may include:

- Do you want a lectern?
- Are you expecting to be on a riser?
- Who else is speaking, or what is happening before and after your presentation?
- What are your lighting preferences?
- Do you need special equipment?
- Does the emcee have a copy of your introduction? (Be sure you have an extra copy.)
- How will you access the stage? From your seat in the audience or from a green room area?
- Do you have a timer, or is there a timer in the audience?
- Do you know the meeting planner's timing expectations if the schedule is off-track when you begin to speak?
- What is your personal microphone preference? A cordless handheld? A lavalier? An ear/mouth piece? A corded handheld? You will always be much more at ease when you work within your comfort zone.

It is important to be in the room well before your scheduled presentation to make any essential changes. This also gives the meeting planner a sense of comfort, knowing there won't be any hectic last-minute adjustments. The goal is to create a peaceful environment for everyone involved!

ELEMENT #3: THE SPEAKER'S CONTENT PREPARATION

Your content should reflect the purpose, objective, or desired outcome of the meeting planner.

When you prepare your presentation, ask yourself these questions:

- What have I been asked to achieve? (The expectations of the meeting planner will provide your answer.)
- Who will be in the audience? (Clarifying every aspect of this question is critical to your content.)
- How much time will you have?
- What other speakers are on the same agenda? (Be clear about their subject matter to avoid duplication.)
- What research do you need to do to understand the history and purpose of this organization, industry, or topic?
- What *personal* experiential knowledge do you have that would fit the needs of the audience?
- What personal stories do you have that illustrate the knowledge you plan to share?

ELEMENT #4: THE SPEAKER'S MESSAGE

Listen to yourself. Listen to your audience, and be aware of their values.

There is an effective pattern that will enhance your eloquence. I call it the PSA—point, story, application—pattern.

Certainly your purpose will vary based on your reason for being there. Are you entertaining? Educating? Inspiring? Training? Motivating? Informing? Regardless of your purpose, your content is best created around the rhythm of PSA: point, story, application.

What are the main truths you want to convey? These will be your *points*. What *story* or illustration will you use to paint a picture that explains these thoughts for your audience? Each point should have at least one story to underscore your message.

Finally, you must determine how an audience member can *apply* what you have said. Every point and story must have an application that will provide value for your audience long after they've left the room.

The PSA approach is bookended by a strong opening and conclusion. Here's a basic outline for your reference:

- **Your opening** is your opportunity to set up the theme or overall direction of your message. (You should have created a snappy or informative title that has given your listeners a sense of your content.)

   The opening can be powerful when you begin with a great story, self-deprecating humor, or a meaningful question. Your purpose is to give the audience time to feel the completeness of your presence with them. Be fully conscious of connecting—with your eyes, your voice, your heart, your purpose for being there.

- **Your primary truths**—your points, stories and application—will be the body of your message. The controlling factors are your underlying purpose and how much time you have.

- **Your closing** wraps up your message. During the conclusion, your goal is to affirm the overall take-away message. This is part of the pattern of eloquence. You are creating an echo, leaving behind a message and value for listeners. One of the most effective means for achieving this is to refer back to your opening story or illustration. This reference then allows you to summarize your key points.

ELEMENT #5: THE SPEAKER'S CONFIDENCE

The greatest element in eloquence is intangible. And that is confidence.

True eloquence is often a by-product of a person's deep awareness of a subject or issue and his or her knowledge of its value and import. This knowledge gives you confidence. And this heightened sense of self can protect you from exhibiting arrogance, egotism, and self-promotion—all antagonists to eloquence.

In addition to your inner confidence, there is tremendous power in being free from preoccupation with yourself. In his book, *The Second Force*, Gary Emery discusses the essence of free-flowing rhythm in any undertaking. He suggests the need to "fall in tune with whatever you're doing." Emery goes on to say that people lose their "natural rhythm" when they get "reversed." He writes, "Look for a feeling of love in whatever you are doing. Love has natural harmony and forward movement to it."

There is tremendous freedom in focusing on connectedness, love, harmony, and being fully present. This is a critical aspect of eloquence through one central focus: Dare to be fully present and connected *off* the platform, every single day, and in every single relationship. Eloquence is a way of living, not simply a way of speaking. To be an authentic, eloquent platform professional requires speakers to focus on being authentic, eloquent human beings.

Known for her spontaneity, humor, and high energy, Glenna Salsbury, CSP, CPAE, Cavett Award recipient, speaks on leadership and customer service in the corporate world. Virtually all of her business is repeat and referral clients. Glenna also coaches professional speakers on how to tap into their authentic voices and deliver their material with eloquence. A graduate of Northwestern University, Glenna holds master's degrees from UCLA and Fuller Seminary. A member of the National Speakers Association since 1980, she received the CPAE Speaker Hall of Fame award in 1990 and was the recipient of NSA's highest honor, the Cavett Award, in 2005. Glenna served as the national president of NSA in 1997-1998. She resides in Paradise Valley, Arizona. Contact her at Glenna@glennasalsbury.com.

WHAT'S YOUR STORY?

Sam Horn

"Stories only happen to people who can tell them."
—L.W. Stanek

A couple of years ago, I was on the closing panel of a conference held over the holidays. The audience included Pulitzer Prize winners, astronauts, Fortune 500 CEOs, nonprofit leaders, and Nobel laureates. This was a big deal.

The challenge? I had two minutes—max—to share an intriguing epiphany with the group.

The night before the panel, my son Andrew came back to our hotel room after some New Year's revelry and found me still working on my remarks. He asked, "What's up, Mom?"

I told him, "Well, I have something to say, but I know it's not special."

"Do what you always tell me to do when I'm studying and I'm too tired to think straight. Get up early in the morning, and the words will come when you're fresh."

Good advice. I set the alarm for 6:00 a.m. and went to bed.

The next morning, I went in search of some caffeine to kick-start my creativity. I turned around after getting my coffee and bumped into a petite powerhouse. I smiled at her and said, "Happy New Year."

She looked at me, eyes bright, and said, *"Start to finish."*

I was instantly intrigued and asked, "How did you come up with that great phrase and philosophy?"

She said, "Want to sit for a spell and I'll tell you?"

I had a decision to make. Was I supposed to go back to my room and work on my two minutes—or was Dr. Betty Siegel my two minutes?

Suffice it to say, I went with Betty.

That conversation not only yielded a fascinating story for my closing remarks, it was the start of a rewarding friendship with the irrepressible Dr. Betty Siegel, President Emeritus of Kennesaw State University and the longest-serving female president of a public university in the nation.

Betty is, quite simply, the best storyteller I've ever known. She doesn't tell; she shows. She illustrates each of her ideas with a vividly told, real-life example so we *see* what she's saying.

Betty is a walking-talking exemplar of the most important insight I've learned in my twenty-plus years as a professional speaker.

People don't want information . . . they want epiphanies. And they don't get epiphanies from information; they get them from examples where the lights go on, the band plays, and someone decides to do something differently.

You may be thinking, "I agree with this, but *how* do I do it?

1. RE-ENACT A REAL-LIFE SITUATION SO IT'S AS IF IT'S HAPPENING . . . *RIGHT NOW.*

A couple of summers ago, I was immersed in writing a book. The weeks flew by, September came, and I never went swimming once.

Yikes. I promised myself that wouldn't happen this summer. I vowed to swim at least three times a week—either in my backyard lake or in one of the twenty-two public pools in our community outside Washington, D.C.

One day, I wrapped up a day of consults and went "pool shopping." I drove past an inviting pool I'd never tried, tucked back under some shade trees. I parked and went in, armed with my goggles for some lapping and a towel for some napping.

As I walked in and saw the fountain in the shallow end packed with kids, moms, and a few dads, I knew I'd found the "family" pool.

As I settled in on the only available deck chair, a father walked in, still in his business suit, and was met with a thrilled chorus of "Daddy!" from his three kids, who ran-walked (lest the lifeguard tweet her whistle) to greet him.

He walked over to the woman on the chair next to me, gave her a peck on the cheek and went to change into his trunks.

Five minutes later he was in the pool, surrounded by his adoring brood, playing Marco Polo. (How comforting to know kids still do that.) The mom watched with a proud smile, probably ready for a break after a day entertaining three kids under the age of six.

The kids were all vying for their dad's attention, "Look at me, look at me," showing the progress they'd made in the strokes they were learning in their swim lessons. He started giving them rides on his shoulders and tossing them into the water, much to their delight.

It did my heart good to watch this Walton-like tableau unfold in front of me. All of a sudden, the father paused for a moment and looked at his wife. He said, almost in a state of wonderment, **"Hon, why don't we make this our default? Why don't we just meet here at the pool every night after work?"**

I have to admit that I held my breath.

I looked at her, thinking, "Please say yes."

She looked at him, smiled in agreement and said, *"Why don't we?"*

That simple decision, which took five seconds to make, could turn this into what everyone remembers as "the summer we met Dad at the pool every afternoon." The summer of no BlackBerry smartphones. The summer everything was right with their world. The summer they gave each other the gift of their time.

What are your defaults? What do you automatically do without thinking?

Are those behaviors helping or hurting you? Could you do something differently today that could reap a lifetime of fond memories—a life of results vs. regrets?

Maybe you could change your default to go for a walk every night after dinner instead of sitting down to watch TV. Enjoy the fireflies instead of a reality show. If you always chair your staff meeting, maybe you could delegate that to one of your staff members next time and give her an opportunity to take the lead.

Choosing to change things up rather than habitually indulging in routine behaviors can have a dramatic, enduring positive impact. Next time you do something that feels viscerally right, ask yourself, "How can I make this my new default so it's an ongoing vs. occasional thing?" Substituting an inspiring behavior for an autopilot behavior can be a stepping stone to the life you're meant to lead.

2. MAKE YOUR EXAMPLE COME ALIVE WITH DIALOGUE AND FIVE-SENSE DETAILS.

Imagine if I stepped on stage and started with, "It's important to try new things." You might have thought, "Boring. Get me out of here."

Reenacting that scene and painting a word picture with back-and-forth dialogue enabled the audience to experience it as if they were right there on the chair next to me. Describing the moment-by-moment unfolding of what happened engaged the audience and kept them on the edge of their seats, wanting to know what the mother said.

Perhaps most importantly, participants approached me after the program and have sent e-mails relating how that story impacted them and how it motivated them to change a default—for the better.

Are you preparing a presentation? If so, instead of starting off with something predictable (which may cause eyes to roll and audiences to break out their BlackBerry smartphones for a distraction), pleasantly surprise your audience by jumping right into a real-life situation that illustrates your point.

Reenact it with dialogue. Describe the scene so we can see it, smell it, hear it. That will make it come alive and cause the audience to fully engage because they are experiencing it as if it's happening right now.

Muriel Rukeyser said, "The world is not made up of atoms; it's made up of stories." Your audience will hang on your every word because they'll be one with your message—they'll feel completely immersed in what you're saying. You'll know you're doing it "right" when there's no shuffling in the seats, no tapping feet, no checking of BlackBerry smartphones. This ideal state of "entrainment" only happens when you reenact a story so realistically, everyone is imagining it in their minds.

3. HOOK AND HINGE YOUR STORY SO LISTENERS APPLY YOUR INSIGHTS TO THEIR SITUATIONS.

Be sure to follow up your story by relating it back to your listeners with questions directed toward them. That's called a "hook and hinge," and it's the surest way to set up two-way communication.

You've probably been to presentations that were one-way monologues. I'll always remember an Olympic athlete who spoke about how he had trained for years, run into many obstacles, but persevered and ultimately won a gold medal. It was impressive, but it was all about him. It was like he was channeling Bette Midler's character in the movie *Beaches*, "Enough about me. What do you think about me?"

At no point did he segue to his listeners and ask, "Have you ever worked hard for a goal? Did you run into obstacles that tempted you to give up? What kept you going? What was it like when you finally achieved your dream?"

From now on, when you finish a story, always extract the key point (the hook) and turn it back to your audience (the hinge) by asking a variation of a "you" question such as, "Where have you encountered this? Is this going on in your life? How are you going to follow up on this idea? How are you going to approach this differently from now on?"

Joseph Conrad wrote that what he was trying to do, "by the power of the written and spoken word," was to make people hear, feel, and—above all—"to make you see."

If you do the above three things the next time you speak, you'll make *your* story *your audience's* story. Audience members will relate to you, remember you, and become your word-of-mouth ambassadors. Perhaps most importantly, they'll be motivated to act on your ideas and will generate real-world benefits because they heard you speak.

If you make your ideas come alive by illustrating them with real-life examples that transform your information into epiphanies, you will make a positive difference in your audience's lives. And, ultimately, isn't that the purpose of speaking?

Sam Horn, The Intrigue Expert, is an award-winning communication strategist/consultant with a 20-year track record of results, with an international clientele including Intel, YPO, Fortune 500 Forum, NASA, KPMG, Cisco, Boeing, and Capital One. Sam is the author of six published books, including *POP! Tongue Fu!* and *What's Holding You Back?* and was named a top-rated speaker at the 2008 *INC Magazine* 500/5000 conference, honoring the top entrepreneurs in the world.

THE IMPACT OF STORIES

Max W. Dixon

Stories have always been a major source of encouragement and inspiration. This is particularly true for speakers, who nurture and develop stories as a vital part of our culture's identity and as a way to entertain, inspire, and influence our listeners. From the time we are children, we love to hear stories about who we are, why we are worth something, how we could do and be better. We love to laugh. We want to play. Perhaps most important of all, we need to illuminate paths of possibility where the way is dimly lit.

Periods of uncertainty and challenge lead to searching for icons of stability—yet they're not always available. Community life, family solidarity, job security, the national economy, and many other traditional sources of comfort may lack the definiteness that human beings crave.

That's when professional speakers have a chance to shine. It's an opportunity to help others see more clearly by sharing stories that reacquaint us with our better selves, remind us of what we have in common and encourage us to come brightly alive with innovation, daring, and laughter.

Most speakers know this already, of course, and seldom does a pro fail to communicate through storytelling. Apart from strategies for improving delivery, the most common questions are these:

- How can I most effectively and efficiently find more stories?
- How can I make them even more involving and more interesting?
- What are the shared ingredients of effective stories, and how can I best craft my stories to be of maximum significance for the audience?

Audiences want solutions to problems. They want guidance and sources they can trust and learn from. They want to hear stories that illuminate a world of greater possibilities. Here's how to accomplish that.

How can we find more stories?

Max's Story Work Sheet (sample included at end of chapter) will help generate the initial material for between 50 and 120 personal stories. They won't be the full stories yet, but rather the reminders of many experiences and clarifiers of the first steps on the way there.

1. On a blank sheet of 8 1/2 x 11 paper, write down the words Conflict, Decision, and Discovery (one line each) in the upper-left corner. Now it's time to create awareness . . . what associated words come to mind? A few examples to get started:

   - Conflict: argument, war, fight, stress . . .

   - Decision: choices, resolutions, difficult, evidence

   - Discovery: invention, transformation, at last, result, eureka!

   Spend about a half-minute on each word just to get the energy of those words floating around in your mind.

   Leaving the other three corners and a small space in the center clear, fill the rest of the page with life roles, activities, self-definitions, silly actions, functional activities—anything that you can think of—that you have done or been. Write without pause for exactly seven minutes. Don't stop to think, and don't leave anything off as "insignificant." If it can be recalled, it's worth writing down—Boy Scout, wife, father, potato-chip fanatic, poet, jumper in water puddle, car buyer. Quantity is the goal.

2. Select either conflict, decision, or discovery for the first round.

3. Close your eyes, hover over the Story Work Sheet with a finger, and let it land on one of the functions/roles/etc. If you chose "decision" and landed on "sweater knitter," that should provoke some kind of mental picture, feeling, or memory.

4. Do that two more times, using whichever you haven't used from conflict, decision, and discovery. Write down all three pairings.

5. If you're working with a partner, each of you will tell the other one what those three pairs are (such as conflict/project manager; decision/dieter; discovery/16th birthday). The other person will respond by asking, "Tell

just a little bit more of a story about . . . " and choose one of the three. (For example, "Tell me a bit more about a decision you made as a dieter.") Then, reverse roles, taking no longer than a half-minute to a full minute describing the experience.

6. For those flying solo in this exercise, pick the most interesting one.

Now look at the upper-right corner of the Story Work Sheet. Here we'll put a basic outline of story construction, specifically "The Hero's Journey." (Classic examples include Joseph Campbell's *The Hero with a Thousand Faces*; Christopher Vogler's *The Writer's Journey*; and Jean Houston's *The Search for the Beloved*, chapter 9, "Of Story and Myth.") In the traditional Hero's Journey, the structure usually contains a protagonist or hero who 1) sets out to accomplish something for a reason, then 2) encounters an obstacle, threat, or conflict 3) from which there may be a way out discovered by that hero, or from another source of real or mysterious origin, with 4) a happy or tragic ending which, either way, imparts new wisdom.

THE HERO'S JOURNEY

- The Call: a want, a goal, a desire
- Obstacles: a conflict that gets in the way of The Call
- Resolution: how the obstacles were met
- New Wisdom: what was learned from the experience

Begin to assemble pairings of function (conflict, decision, discovery) and role —as many as possible—by writing one sentence for each Hero's Journey function for each story.

For example, if the pairing was "conflict/played cornet in H.S. marching band," the result would be:

- **The Call:** I wanted to be really good at playing my cornet while I was marching with the band on the field during halftime at football games.
- **Obstacles:** I was simply awful at holding the mouthpiece on my lips, not banging my teeth with it, counting the steps, keeping the rows and files straight, playing music.

- **Resolution:** I found a simple way I could change in how I walked, then how I breathed and so on, until I could do it all.

- **New Wisdom:** I found that reducing my first step to a tiny target helped it appear, feel, and be manageable.

How can I make my stories more involving and interesting?

Of the memories, events, and recollections, filled with conflicts, decisions and discoveries, some are clearly more significant or "stickier" than others. These are the ones worth shaping into stories—and thus learning experiences and teaching points on their way to improving lives or transforming a corporation.

Every person who writes about or coaches storytelling offers a slightly different set of guidelines on how to make a story more involving. It's worth examining a lot of them—and coming to appreciate the commonalities rather than the differences.

The goal, whether using the Hero's Journey or any other framework, is to have an audience remember stories in a way that influences their behavior. Cognitive science tells us that we are more likely to be affected by material that arouses feelings, suggests meaning, and offers a helpful pattern in its structure. Interesting, relevant, remembered . . . qualities designed to assist a story be inspiring and enduring.

The most powerful stories have the following traits:

1. A setting and place that support the action and ignite the senses.

    Where something occurs provides context that supports vivid pictures. This drops the listeners' defenses and begins their engagement in the story's action. Assemble more details about the environment than needed, and edit down to the essentials.

2. Characters we find interesting and whom we want to see survive.

    Many stories fail because the characters aren't emotionally interesting. What do they want? What do they care about? Can we identify with those values and desires? How do they move and act? Let's see them doing something that reveals an attitude. Use strong, graphic verbs. Provide illustrations that include descriptions of activity. Rather than "My uncle was so polite," a storyteller would say, "My uncle would always offer a smile, gently touch the brim of his hat and say 'good morning' as he walked briskly downtown. The consummate gentleman."

People, places, and things need to have character depth. It starts with names for neighbors, buildings, bridges, dogs, values, events—because listeners can relate only to the specific. Mrs. Steuhrk, Legion Field, the Aurora Bridge, Sheehan of Maghera Glass, faith in Mr. Hanna's integrity, the Schweitzerfest. Sensory language and actualities hit home; impersonal generalities don't. Voice qualities, word choice, postures and gestures all build audience interest and involvement. People want someone to root for—and if they have a sense of humor, it's an opportunity for a story to relax tension.

3. Mysteries we want solved.

Everyone enjoys a bit of intrigue or glimpses of something unknown—a question whose answer would shed light on something that matters. Part of the story may be a search for a quality. How do we find it? Or a solution to a crisis that needs a change in strategy in order to succeed. Build the mystery. Raise the stakes. Intensify the need.

4. Conflicts and tensions we want resolved.

The key to success of many stories, conflict requires great attention to incrementally building the intensity of the opposing forces. It's where we can shine the spotlight on a moment that depends on a decision, an ability, or an insight. Look to have the tension or the conflict resolution come at the point that it provides the point of the story.

For example, this speech imagery allows me to draw the metaphor to how my clients could find it in themselves to offer appreciation to others even in trying times:

> Standing over my 90-year-old father's hospital bed after his heart attack, watching him open his eyes and hearing his first words express his appreciation for my presence and then quoting Shakespeare, showed me how someone "flat on his back" and "whose heart had just about given up" could find the resources to step into my story. And if he could do that . . .

How can I best craft my stories to be of maximum significance to the audience and be highly influential?

Bringing depth and relevance to a story are essential to influencing clients to change their lives for the better. How do we do this? I call it the Transferable Metaphor—connecting the story to the listeners' lives. From the beginning, shape the story toward fulfilling audience needs. Metaphors need to link with their lives in a way that gives them new wisdom and likelihood of survival, however they might define that term. Here, as always, specificity is the heart of credibility.

I mentioned earlier that I say in my speech, my father was "flat on his back" and his "heart was giving out." His first words upon opening his eyes and seeing me were from Shakespeare's *Merchant of Venice,* Act V: "How far that little candle throws his beams! So shines a good deed in a naughty world." And then he said, "Now, I know Portia says that and you're playing Shylock, but thank you so much for coming."

I then say to the audience, "What a guy. At perhaps the most vulnerable moment in his life, he found the energy and heroic capacity to step into my story and elevate my spirits."

The point of the story: There is great power in showing someone that we understand and value their story, that we appreciate their efforts to meet a challenge, and that we are available to assist them if our service would be appropriate.

Then it requires applying the words directly to the corporate/professional/personal context of the audience: "Have we ever felt the heart might be going out of our business . . . that we might be flat on our back? What client or prospective client could we call and ask if our work together is still active in their plans and would they appreciate our attention to their current situation?"

Never make a story about the loss. It's always about the possibilities. Find the action that reflects new wisdom, the smart move, or a plan of action. Uncover the double meaning that applies metaphorically to the audience. Use fully sensory language. Repeat key words as often as it is appropriate. Work in a callback of the point of the story as a reminder into the last thirty seconds of your speech—and, executed properly, it will be remembered long afterward.

Max Dixon's Story Work Sheet

Conflict   *Hero's Journey*
Decision   The Call
Discovery   Obstacles
                                          Resolution
                                          New Wisdom

                          Transferable
                          Metaphor

The Body   *Values*
Senses   1.
Body in the Story   2.
  Story in the Body   3.
Time
Space

Max Dixon is an international keynote speaker and professional communication coach. For 31 years, he was a university teacher of acting, movement, voice, pantomime, improvisation, public speaking, and persuasion that concluded with six years as one of the three core teachers in the Professional Actor Training Program at the University of Washington, School of Drama in Seattle, Washington. As an actor, his focus was on Shakespeare, including roles in which he appeared as guest artist with the Colorado Shakespeare Festival and for Auburn University.

His enthusiastic clients are found among professional speakers, attorneys, financial advisors, executives, artists, and athletes. His highly regarded presentations are *Potency on the Platform: Take Your Body With You* (given for all the NSA chapters), *The Power of Story in a Corporate Setting*, and *Depth Perception: Taking Your Message to Another Level*.

WHEN PRESENTING BECOMES FACILITATING

Kristin Arnold, MBA, CFP, CMC, CSP

Today's audiences don't want a talking head. They want to be engaged in the content, interacting not only with the speaker, but with each other. For the professional speaker, that may require transitioning from idea presentation to discussion facilitation. The facilitator focuses on the process of the session, rather than the content, as the group moves from current reality to desired outcome.

Facilitation, be forewarned, is not for the faint of heart. In its highest form, facilitation expects the participants to drive the agenda while the facilitator helps navigate. This requires more than a usual amount of "letting go," and often takes more time than a conventional presentation. Facilitation requires trust in the process and trust in the group to be able to figure out what they need to hear, say, and do.

In addition to presentation skills, an effective process facilitator typically assumes the following fundamental roles, abilities, and skills:

- Guides the process, including agenda, time limits, and keeping the session on topic.
- Ensures a safe environment that's conducive to collaboration.
- Tees up the discussion, setting the context or goal and sharing how the group will achieve the objective.
- Manages participation, tactfully preventing anyone from being overlooked or dominating the discussion.

- Manages conflict constructively to generate light rather than heat around the point of contention.
- Checks decisions and clarifies next steps, such as specific tasks and deadlines for participants.
- Summarizes discussions and confirms mutual understanding before moving on.
- Intervenes when the group gets off track or if the discussion fragments into multiple conversations.

STEP 1: CLARIFY THE OBJECTIVES.

Typically, a facilitated session is one meeting among a series of meetings. For a facilitator, one of the first challenges is to clarify the overarching goal for the series of meetings, as well as the specific meeting at hand. This includes research on the audience, as well as collaboration with the meeting planner or other interested stakeholders.

STEP 2: BUILD THE AGENDA.

A basic agenda is similar to a presenter's outline; however, the focus is more on the topics for discussion rather than topics to be presented. A typical agenda consists of some opening activities, topical discussions, and closing activities.

1. Open the Meeting
   Establish/Review Agenda
   Icebreaker Activity

2. Topic #1
   Introduce Topic
   Discussion

3. Topic #2
   Introduce Topic
   Discussion

4. Close the Meeting
   Summarize Key Understandings & Next Steps
   Critique

STEP 3: CREATE AN ENGAGING PROCESS.

At a macro level, all group conversations start with a free-flow discussion that generates ideas, problems, causes, solutions, etc., but the brainstorming doesn't stop there! From the generated list of possibilities, the group must somehow organize them in order to make a decision. Finally, once a decision has been made, the group needs to take action. I call this the GODA process: generate, organize, decide, and act.

Generate	Quantity		
Organize	Sort		
	Prioritize		
Decide	Agree		
Act	Plan		

G—Generate a List

Start a brainstorming session by writing the topic on an easel or whiteboard visible to all. Three different methods are typically used to work everyone into the brainstorming process:

1. Freewheel. Anyone on the team can call out an idea, with one person (generally the facilitator) capturing the ideas on an easel chart.

2. Round Robin. Go around the room so that each person has a chance to contribute a new idea or "hitchhike" on a previous idea. Each person has the option to pass. You can switch to freewheeling as more participants pass.

3. Slip. Encourage all of the participants to write down in large and legible letters each of their ideas on a separate slip of paper, sticky note, or index card. A great side benefit of writing each idea separately is that team members are expressing their ideas in their own words and in as much detail as they like.

Have the recorder write all ideas on the easel chart so that all can visualize— or post the sticky notes or index cards on the wall. Continue until the group has exhausted its ideas on the topic or time has run out. Clarify and combine similar ideas, with the permission of the team.

Brainstorming Ground Rules

- All ideas are valid. Any idea is acceptable, even if it seems silly, strange, or similar to a previous idea.

- Participants should say "pass" if they don't have an idea on their turn.

- The process continues until everyone contributes or passes or a predetermined time limit runs out.

- A person will be assigned to capture ideas on an easel or whiteboard.

- Participants are encouraged to add other ideas, otherwise known as "hitchhiking."

- No praise, no comments, no criticism. It's brainstorming!

- Everyone participates . . . no one dominates.

- Start on time; stop on time.

- Misspelling is okay.

- What's said here, stays here.

O—Organize the List

Now it's time to organize the ideas, using one of three different methods:

1. Synthesize. You can summarize what has been said by synthesizing all the ideas into a handful of headlines or highlights.

2. Sort. You can have the group sort the ideas into a few manageable categories or in a specific flow, for example, chronological, process, along a continuum, and so forth.

3. Prioritize. You can have the group narrow the pool of ideas into a smaller, prioritized list.

Once all of the ideas are up on the wall or on the table, they are now the team's ideas. Ask the group to silently (no talking!) sort the ideas under predetermined headings or to cluster them around similar ideas. If a team member doesn't like where an idea note or card has been placed, he or she can move it rather than discuss it.

After the flurry of activity, give a ten-second countdown for all ideas to be settled into their clusters. Categorizing or grouping the ideas into an affinity diagram creates the same result: several categories or headers with several cards underneath each one.

Having organized the large brainstorming list, the team may decide to focus on one or two high-priority categories or to divide into sub-teams to look at each category in more detail. A "quick vote" can help prioritize—just ask the group, "Of all the things we have just considered, what is your top priority?" Go around the room and capture their responses with checkmarks on the list. For a larger group with a larger list, the "multivote" can help pare things down:

1. Ask if anyone needs clarification of an item, or if any two items are so similar they should be combined. If the majority of the group agrees, with no strident objections, then combine them.

2. Participants have ten votes each. They can place all ten votes on one item or they can scatter their ten votes among the many items. (If the list is more than thirty items, it's OK to give team members additional votes.)

3. Ask participants to silently vote by writing item choices and the number of votes on a piece of paper. It's easiest to letter each item, starting with A, B, and so on down the chart, then have team members simply write the letter and the number of votes for each: For instance, A-3, F-2, H-2, I-2, and L-1. To tally, ask the participants to raise the number of fingers for the number of votes they placed on each item. If privacy is an issue, ask the participants to write each of their items and the corresponding

vote on small, separate sticky notes. Turn the easel away from the audience and have individuals come up and vote before adding up the totals.

Note: There may be some vocal members who will want to take the top vote and declare it the "winner." But the reality is that less than 50 percent of the group may have voted for the top vote-getter. This process is designed to identify the top ideas, not the single best idea.

D—Decide Which Ideas to Pursue.

With the list pared down to five or so items, perhaps an obvious option leaps out of the pack and the group comes to a quick decision. Most of the time, however, they are faced with a choice among many options.

If the group is interested and has the time, it can combine, create, and synergize the items into a better idea. Consensus means more than "I can live with it." It means that each person can live with and support the decision upon implementation. Here are steps that can help build a consensus:

1. Explain what consensus means and why it is important for the group to reach one. Clearly outline any constraints (e.g., time or money). Remind each member to participate fully in the discussion. Finally, identify a fallback option (majority vote or command decision) if consensus can't be reached within a specified time.
2. Take the most important items from the smaller list, category headers, or ideas within a category and ask a few probing questions, such as these:
   - "All of these items are possible. Do we have to choose only one, or can we use the best features of each?"
   - "What would happen if we took the added/deleted features of several options? Would that get us closer to what we want?"
   - "Could we try out several options in parallel before we commit to just one?"

This trial-and-error approach may appear chaotic at first, but it's a good way to build a new, synergistic alternative based on the best of the best.

3. When it appears the group has agreed to a new alternative, take a straw poll to see how close the team is to reaching a consensus. Statements

such as these can help:

- "It sounds like we're making progress. Let's check that out with a quick straw poll to see how close we are to a consensus. We'll go right around the table. Sally?"
- "Let's see if everyone can either agree with or agree to support the most popular alternative. Start with Sally and go around the room."

Record the responses and summarize the results. If everyone can live with and support the alternative, then you have a consensus. What if there's still a deadlock? Try something like:

- "There seems to be a lot of support for this alternative. What would it take for the rest of us to support this?"
- "What is getting in the way of some team members supporting this alternative? What could we do to meet their needs?"

Continue to build agreement for the decision until there's a consensus, or time runs out and your team falls back to another decision-making method. A consensus offers the best odds of a quality decision, a more cohesive team, and smoother implementation of the decision.

A—Act on Your Ideas.

A few years ago, I was asked to observe a CEO while he was meeting with his direct reports. After a robust discussion about website strategy, it appeared that they had agreed to a handful of great ideas. After the meeting was over, I asked the CEO, "So, who is going to take action on these great ideas?" The CEO stared at me, believing that one of his VPs would pick up the ball. When I queried the VPs who were at the meeting, they each assumed someone else was going to take the lead.

As a result, nothing got done—until the next meeting.

Accountability is even more important in a facilitated session because the group itself owns the result. If there is no action, the session is a waste of everyone's time. Here are a few techniques to ensure momentum after the meeting:

1. Record possible actions. Have an easel chart ready to record ideas as they emerge, as well as the name of the person who suggested the task.

2. Review actions. At the end of the meeting, make sure the group thoroughly understands the action plan tasks and the scope of the work. You may discover a task doesn't need to be done at all!

3. Confirm responsibility. Confirm the name of at least one person responsible for completing each task. It doesn't mean doing all of the work, but marshalling the right people and resources to get the job done.

4. Check for help. Ask the person responsible if he is going to need some help, and then quickly identify who will help him.

5. Set a specific due date and time. By being specific, the task becomes much more tangible and can be written on each participant's calendar. If appropriate, put the task on a timeline and show how it affects other events or tasks.

6. Document. Capture the action items in meeting minutes and send them out within two days of the meeting.

7. Just do it. Once the commitment has been made, it is up to the individuals to do their fair share—and for the group to hold them accountable. As a facilitator, this action planning creates a structure for follow up to happen.

PREVENTION STRATEGIES

It's almost time to get that meeting started . . . but there's one more checkpoint once the agenda and GODA process are in place. Take a moment to consider Murphy's Law—"Whatever can go wrong, will go wrong"—and ask your sponsor or client what the potential pitfalls are. Take their concerns, add them to your own experience and intuition, and develop your prevention strategies:

1. Clarify the goal. At the beginning of your session, ensure you have agreement on the goal, the agenda/process, and the deliverable. (Don't forget to have a Plan "B" tucked away in your back pocket, in case of Murphy's Law.)

2. Define roles. Facilitators don't have to do it all—what can the participants do? From time-keepers to note-takers, people become more committed to the outcome the more involved they are.

3. Record what is being said. Writing something down provides legitimacy to the idea. Paraphrasing is OK, but make sure the main idea has been correctly captured. Then it can be pointed to, referred to, modified, and saved for posterity.

4. Three-knock rule. Simply knock your knuckle or a pen on the table three times if the discussion starts to wander. Whoever is speaking should stop and refocus on the topic.

5. Use the parking lot. Create a separate easel or board to capture important ideas that aren't relevant to the topic at hand. (Just make sure to come back to it before the end of the meeting.)

6. Agree on how to make decisions. As a general rule, the more interaction, the better the decision will be. For important issues, most organizations strive for consensus . . . with a fallback option, just in case the group can't get there in the allotted period of time.

7. Document the event. Clients want to take action as soon as possible. To help them get a running start, facilitators need to document what transpired during the session and feed it back: transcribe the easel charts, transcribe the conversations, or capture the data on audio or video.

With clear objectives, a defined process agenda for brainstorming, and prevention strategies in place for what could go wrong, 80 percent of the facilitator's work has been done. Yes, it is a tremendous amount of work to prepare for a successful session, but every minute of preparation increases the odds of making it happen—whether the team ends up following the GODA process or Plan "B."

Kristin Arnold, MBA, CPF, CMC, CSP, is one of North America's most accomplished professional meeting facilitators. A consummate author, speaker, and trainer, she is on a crusade to make all events in the workplace more engaging, interactive, and collaborative. One of the first women to graduate from the U.S. Coast Guard Academy and the only woman stationed onboard a Coast Guard buoy tender, Kristin learned firsthand how to build high-performance teams, engage others in the workplace, and get the job done. She earned an MBA from St. Mary's College of California and teaches teambuilding at the Schulich School of Business at York University in Toronto. Kristin divides her time between Phoenix, Arizona, and Prince Edward Island, Canada. Visit www.extraordinaryteam.com.

FACILITATION 101: THE SIX ROLES OF EFFECTIVE FACILITATORS

Jonathan Tessier

In learning circles, a lot of terms get thrown around to describe the role of teacher: instructor, educator, speaker, presenter, and commonly today, facilitator. So, what exactly is a facilitator? And just how does this role differ from the other versions of teaching? For speakers who want to expand into the world of training and conducting programs for adults, it's important to know how a facilitator functions in the classroom.

In the 21st century world of training, it is no longer sufficient to stand at the front of the room and present information to a passive audience. Instead, discussions, interactions, and learner-centered activities are in demand. That's precisely what a facilitator does—create learning from what's talked about or experienced by participants rather than solely what the teacher has to say.

Facilitators certainly may bring an expertise to their training program; indeed, it's important that they can speak credibly around the topic of their training. But with facilitation, the emphasis is less on presenting a large amount of information and more on how people are talking about and learning from what is being discussed among them. This interaction and sharing of opinions, perspectives, and experiences is what can make a training program a unique and powerful experience. The facilitator simply offers participants opportunities to interact with one another and to learn, based on whatever comes up during the training.

The skilled facilitator accomplishes this through six key roles that he or she performs during any training program.

ROLE #1: THE FACILITATOR CREATES A SAFE ENVIRONMENT FOR LEARNING TO TAKE PLACE.

Creating a safe environment means that the facilitator makes sure that every participant feels comfortable—allowing them to open up and let learning happen during training. Many adults typically feel insecure at the start of a training program, because they don't necessarily like to admit that there is something they don't already know. After all, aren't we supposed to have all the answers? Isn't that what defines adulthood? If that is the perceived truth, the mere presence in a training room suggests that we don't have all the answers—a tacit admission that can make someone feel a bit vulnerable.

So, the facilitator must first remove the conscious and unconscious blocks that adults bring with them to a training program that can inhibit their ability to fully learn. It's up to the facilitator to make sure everyone feels comfortable in the classroom and to replace any negative feelings and assumptions about learning with positive assumptions—clearing the way for a learning experience.

The facilitator also needs to plant the seeds for learning success, letting participants know that the outcome of the training is going to be positive. Indirectly, the facilitator is letting participants know that there's nothing to be concerned or worried about during the training program. No one will be put on the spot or be made to feel inferior. On the contrary, everyone will meet with success and be thankful for having come to the program. When the facilitator creates a mind-set of success for the participants from the outset, it works to ease apprehension and loosen up participants so that they can be ready to jump in and learn.

Finally, the facilitator can help create a safe environment by letting participants know specifically what will be covered during the training and the benefits participants will gain from the course. "What's in it for me?" continues to ring true. Adults have a basic need to know the purpose of the training and what they will be able to do as a result of what they will learn. Establishing the benefits up front will engage the participants' hearts as well their minds. Understanding the benefits of the training will also prepare participants to apply the lessons to their lives. It will humanize the learning into something warm, touchable, inspirational, and personally motivating. Knowing this will allow participants to make the conscious choice of investing their effort into the training program, because they already know that something of value waits for them at the end.

Keep in mind, though, that learner's benefits cannot simply be delivered in rote fashion to the participants. Instead, the participants must establish these benefits for themselves. It is the participants who have to determine what will be valuable to them. Only the participant knows best what the payoff will be. Therefore, it is essential at the beginning of the training to have participants identify what they hope to gain, so that they can personally connect to the topic right from the beginning.

ROLE #2: THE FACILITATOR STIMULATES THE PARTICIPANT'S THINKING.

Participants need to be immersed in the learning for it to be most effective, and they will be stimulated in their thinking if they are allowed to discover information rather than being spoon-fed. Again, if you think about the traditional methods of classroom teaching, participants are passively receiving information. But content is not something that a participant merely consumes; rather, it is something they actually create. Only what participants physically do, talk about with others, and reflect upon can be converted into true, usable knowledge.

In this technically and electronically advanced world, people are continually bombarded with information, and their brains are constantly filtering through a vast volume of information. As a result, facilitators must eliminate lecturing as the primary means of delivering information in a training program. Typically, lecturing allows for more information to be covered in a shorter amount of time, which is one of the main reasons it continues to live on. However, if participants are not actively engaged in the training, it's a pretty good bet they are not learning.

Lecturing, for the most part, is not learner-centered. It is far more effective to have a training program that utilizes a variety of methods for delivering content. If lecturing *is* used, it must be combined with visual aids, interactive, hands-on activities, and other ways to involve participants.

ROLE #3: THE FACILITATOR INVOLVES THE PARTICIPANT IN THE LEARNING PROCESS.

There's an adage that guides the facilitator's approach to training: "Never do for learners what learners can do for themselves." What this means is that the facilitator must use every opportunity to hand over control of the learning to participants. Any opportunity to turn something passive into something active will benefit the participants' learning and help them to turn information into retainable knowledge.

Learning is the formation of new meanings from existing information. Practically speaking, learning happens when participants are allowed to speak with one another, discuss a situation, or reflect upon new ideas or the perspectives being generated in their own minds. Learning happens when participants share their thoughts and feelings, hopes, and concerns, as well as their real-world experiences surrounding a topic. The more a facilitator can get participants to take notes, ask questions, fill in blanks in a workbook, illustrate an idea using colored markers, or present their ideas in front of the class, the more likely the information will convert into knowledge that participants will find useful.

Whatever the facilitator can do, however big or small, to make learning an active process for participants rather than a passive consumption of information will increase the potential for an engaging and successful training program. Still, it's a challenge for most teachers to approach training in this way, because it means letting go of the reins of the program and letting participants exercise the freedom to create what will work best for them. This also means that the facilitator must trust that whatever comes up during an activity is what needs to happen, no matter how much it deviates from some preset agenda.

ROLE #4: THE FACILITATOR MANAGES THE LEARNING PROCESS.

When the facilitator manages the learning process, he or she lets the program expand as needed in certain areas, while allowing it to compress in others where the learning has happened more quickly than expected. This ebb and flow takes a great deal of discernment on the part of the facilitator, who must constantly take the pulse of the class, monitor participant energy levels, and adjust accordingly.

Managing the learning process and creating flow in a training program requires a facilitator to quietly modify the training program's agenda. Managing the learning process, therefore, also suggests that the facilitator must know and understand what type of people make up the training program's audience. A facilitator pays attention to the character clues that participants project about learning types, sociability, and initial perspectives on the training program's topic. It is vital that the facilitator honor, each and every participant.

The overall goal of the facilitator is to make it easy for participants to learn. Whatever will work for participants needs to be recognized and supported, which may include abandoning the program's agenda altogether in favor of going in a completely different direction—if that's what's best for the participants. It's a bit of a juggling act, and it takes a great deal of observation by the facilitator to recognize the little clues indicating what the participants need. Remember, it's not about being a subject matter expert first and foremost. Instead, it's about creating the conditions and being flexible enough to allow for the best learning experience.

ROLE #5: THE FACILITATOR ENSURES INDIVIDUAL PARTICIPANT ACCOUNTABILITY.

Participants, not the facilitator, are responsible for their own learning, and they play a crucial role in making learning happen. By letting participants know that you are paying attention and that it's not acceptable for anyone to be nonparticipative in the training program, it sends an important message that you genuinely care about individuals and want to ensure that everyone takes away as much learning as possible.

Participants have to participate. Facilitators are responsible for facilitating, and making sure that learning is happening and they're doing everything in their power to make that so. Of course, they can't get people to learn if they don't want to, but the facilitator can offer resistant participants every opportunity to join in.

ROLE #6: THE FACILITATOR TIES IT ALL TOGETHER FOR THE PARTICIPANT.

The facilitator is like an adventure guide, who not only takes participants on an educational and entertaining journey but also safely brings them back to the point where their journey first began. The same is true in effectively designed training programs, which always end at the same place they began, with participants having grown along the way. So, at the end of the training program, the facilitator summarizes the learning and ties it all together.

Like the final chapter of a story, the facilitator also communicates what will happen for participants after the training program is over. Remember, the end of a training program does not have to be the end of the relationship between the facilitator and the participants. In fact, it's often just the beginning. Facilitators are encouraged to use their training programs as a way to educate and inform on an ongoing basis and to develop relationships that will lead to opportunities in the future. The training program can be the start of a long-term relationship, so it is important to have ways to maintain contact over time. Facilitators need to realize that they can continue to serve participants by offering additional products and services that extend the value far beyond the final minute of the training program.

DON'T DELIVER KNOWLEDGE . . . CREATE IT.

Perhaps the most important goal for a facilitator during training is connecting with people. Face it, participants can obtain a lot of information from many sources outside a training program. But only a facilitator can bring people together, touch their lives in profound ways, and provide them with a unique learning experience. So, call yourself a teacher, instructor, presenter, speaker, or trainer if you simply want to deliver information in a learning program. By becoming a facilitator, you can make participants actively involved in creating knowledge that can significantly alter their lives.

Jonathan Tessier is a senior instructional designer for Ready2Go Training Solutions. He is a successful training manager, professional coach, and award-winning instructional designer. Jonathan holds a master's degree in education with an emphasis in training and development, and a bachelor's degree in film & communications. He also has two professional coaching certifications, which he currently uses to promote positive employee performance and career success. Visit www.Ready2GoTraining Solutions.com.

A PAUSE CAN BUILD APPLAUSE

Lou Heckler, CSP, CPAE

Speakers are word people, filling time and space with stories and concepts—but in the process, it's easy to ignore one of the most effective tools at a speaker's disposal: silence. Pausing can add a great deal to the audience's enjoyment, comprehension, and appreciation of presentations. There are three prime areas to consider as opportunities for pauses.

TIME TO THINK

If there is one mistake I see speakers (including me) make repeatedly, it is trying to cover too much material. To make matters worse, speakers rarely get the full-time allotment for which they have been hired. Attendees show up late because they have trouble finding parking . . . the association president's message runs long . . . the coffee break takes more time than anticipated . . . and everything gets backed up all day. *Have no fear,* thinks the meeting planner. *The professional speaker will get things back on time.* And we usually do.

That fact alone might be a good motivation for taking less material to the platform. More important, audiences need time to think and consider what a speaker is offering. Often, I am asked what the primary difference is between a workshop and a keynote speech. While they share some common elements, I explain it this way: Workshops teach skills, and speeches are designed to prompt thinking. In either case, audience members need time to consider what's being said, weigh it against what they already know, and evaluate it in the context of their careers and their lives. The pause offers that chance.

One effective way to use the pause in this context is to combine it with some stage movement. Consider making your key point, and then pausing as you walk from one side of the stage or staging area to the other. Look at the audience, perhaps nod gently, cueing them that this is a good time to let that idea sink in. When you start your next segment, their brains won't feel rushed.

We can also do this with your eyes. I was watching an episode of the Bravo Cable TV show *Inside the Actors Studio* one evening, and Academy Award winner Michael Caine was the sole guest. Host James Lipton asked him, "What's the biggest difference between acting on stage and acting on film?'

Caine replied, "Actually, they're very similar." He placed one of his hands above his eyes and the other just below and said, "It's all here. Everything you wish to convey to the audience has to show up in your eyes, because that's where people are looking." So, too, for the speaker: When pausing to prompt the audience to think about a point, your eyes must convey that you are thinking about it as well.

Here's what I always imagine is taking place. I tell a story or anecdote, and then I pause. Inside the audience members' brains, there's a silent response to what I've just said: "Right . . . my dad always said that was true," or "Yes! My seventh-grade English teacher (or coach, pastor, priest, or rabbi) used to say that." In essence, they are validating the message by realizing that they already know this fact or idea, though they hadn't consciously thought about it for a while. By pairing the new idea with the "old" learning, something very good happens: They embrace your point on a personal level.

So, how much time is appropriate to allot for thinking time? I routinely write or prepare about two-thirds to three-fourths of the time I have been given. I have come to believe that participants learn more when we give them a lot about a little, instead of a little about a lot.

TIME TO ANTICIPATE

I once asked a child psychologist, "What is something about children that most of us forget?"

"That's easy . . . kids love to anticipate," he responded. "Every day, every child should have some event to look forward to in the short term and in the long term."

As I moved into the speaking business from a corporate job in broadcasting, I recalled his statement and thought to myself, "I think this is true for adults as well. Aren't we all still just children in big people's clothing?"

Television game shows play anticipation to the hilt. A player answers, and the host pauses before saying if the answer is correct or not. The delay builds suspense and gives viewers the chance to consider (and perhaps second-guess) their own answers.

Audiences want to feel like they're part of the presentation, not necessarily by voicing an audible answer, but by feeling like they are in a mental dialogue with the speaker. This seems especially true when it comes to humor. Much of what we laugh about either takes us completely by surprise or the exact opposite—something you can see coming from a mile away, so it's like you're in on the punch line. If you know you have a great line to end a story or an example, pause a few beats before delivering it and watch how much more fun the audience has savoring the line.

Another way to use the pause to build anticipation is to plant an idea early in the presentation and keep circling back to it. A few years ago, while I was doing a multiple-day seminar, a skeptic in the room was not enamored with my ideas about creative problem solving. I heard him saying, "Yeah, right!" under his breath to the other people at his table.

With a last name like mine, I'm well aware of how to handle a heckler. I told the group, "Some of my ideas today may seem a little far out to you. Although I think this is part of what stimulates creativity, I know some of you feel it's not very bottom-line-oriented." I told them if that happened throughout the day, they should feel free to yell out, "Yeah, right!"

For sixty minutes, no one made a peep. Anticipation was building. I felt I had to get things going, so when someone answered one of my questions with a pretty "fuzzy" idea, I paused, looked around the room, grinned, and blurted, "Yeah, right!" The crowd roared their approval, the floodgates were opened for the rest of the day, and it stopped Mr. Skeptic in his tracks.

On the final day, as I was wrapping up, a man raised his hand at the back of the room. "Lou," he said, "earlier this week, I think many of us thought your ideas were a little impractical, but I think I can speak for everyone when I say that this was one of the most helpful sessions I have ever attended, and I know we will all think differently and more creatively from now on."

I was touched by the heartfelt praise, not even sure how to respond. Of course, just as I opened my mouth to voice my thanks, the whole room exploded in a huge, "Yeah, right!" It was a magical moment, enhanced by several days of anticipation.

TIME TO INTERNALIZE

At the end of a seminar I did for a senior citizens group on the healing power of humor, a woman came up to me when the room had almost emptied out. She took my hands in hers and said, "My husband died seven months ago. Today is the first day I have been able to laugh." What a gift she gave me—and what a reminder that all audience members are there for their own reasons, equipped with their own perspectives and motivations, and with their own need to internalize your message.

One of my favorite examples of giving time to internalize comes from a professional speaker associate of mine. He tells the story of a friend whose wife passed away from cancer in her forties. On the morning of the afternoon funeral, he felt he needed to do something out of ordinary to show his love and concern for the widowed husband.

He took one of his children's shoeshine kits—a little wooden box with a slanted top— and he went to the man's door. After a heartfelt greeting, he asked the man, "What shoes will you be wearing to the funeral today?" The man was a bit flabbergasted by the question. "My black ones, I guess," he finally said. "Bring them out," my associate said, "And put them on."

As he knelt at the man's feet, shining away like a skilled pro at a barbershop, the man opened up to him. He expressed his deep sorrow and his fears of inadequacy raising his children alone . . . and his appreciation for what was happening at that moment.

In the retelling of this story, my associate then turns to the audience and says, "Whose shoes do you need to shine today?" And he pauses, for a fairly prolonged period, allowing people to process the metaphor it contained for them and their lives. It is a story that begs not to be rushed. And it is a testimony to the power of the pause as a way to enhance a presentation—en route to the bigger picture of transforming the way people think, act, and feel.

Lou Heckler, CSP, CPAE, divides his professional time between delivering keynote speeches on leadership, peak performance, and engagement and coaching other professional speakers in material organization and presentation skills. Reach him at Lou@LouHeckler.com or at www.LouHeckler.com.

IMPROV RULES!
FIVE WAYS TO MAKE YOUR
SPEECHES MORE POWERFUL
AND ENGAGING

Gilda Bonanno

Imagine stepping out onto the stage of Gotham City Improv in New York City. The house lights are dark, the stage lights are on, and you stare into the darkness where the audience is seated. You feel a thrill of excitement and a rush of anxiety.

The director speaks to the audience: "I need an occupation for the people on stage," and several responses come back: "spelunkers . . . doctors . . . astronauts . . . plumbers . . ." He selects the first one he heard, and shouts "Begin scene!" Suddenly, you and the other person on stage are spelunkers.

As its name suggests, improvisational comedy (improv for short) is completely spontaneous—without scripts, dress rehearsals, or preplanned outlines of a scene. Once you're on stage, you could be piloting an alien spaceship, drinking cocktails with Hollywood stars, or dancing the tango with your kindergarten teacher.

As a professional speaker, you can apply key lessons from improv comedy to increase your confidence, enhance your stage presence, allow you to interact with the audience more effectively, and make your speeches more creative.

Despite its improvised nature, improv comedy has specific rules and requires practice. Team members practice by doing exercises and getting feedback to improve fundamental improv skills. The improv comedy rules provide structure and create the environment in which creativity can flourish.

Although many Americans associate improv comedy with the TV show *Whose Line Is It Anyway?*, it actually goes back to the 1930s when Viola Spolin developed theatrical improvisation. She wrote the classic book on improv, *Improvisation for the Theater*, first published in 1963. Theater troupes such as Second City and the Committee pioneered improv comedy, and others such as the Groundlings, Upright Citizens Brigade, and many more developed it further.

An improv show consists of short scenes created by two or more actors based on audience suggestions. Short-form improv consists of stand-alone scenes that are not linked, while long-form improv links the various scenes by a common thread.

Not all comedy is primarily improvisational. For example, you're undoubtedly familiar with stand-up comedy, which involves one comedian on stage with a microphone, telling a set of written, memorized, and rehearsed jokes. You've also probably watched sketch comedy, made famous by television's *Saturday Night Live*, which consists of written and rehearsed scenes, though performers may improvise some lines during the live performance.

Here are five improv comedy rules that can help professional speakers connect to the audience and deliver speeches that are more powerful and engaging.

RULE #1: EXPECT THE UNEXPECTED.

Improv comedy is all about expecting the unexpected. Because nothing in the scene is planned, you have to be fully in the moment and responsive to the audience's suggestions and your fellow actors. That spontaneity can feel terrifying at first, but eventually it can be liberating. In the words of Viola Spolin, spontaneity

> creates an explosion that for the moment frees us from handed-down frames of reference, memory choked with old facts, and information and undigested theories and techniques of other people's findings. Spontaneity is the moment of personal freedom when we are faced with a reality and see it, explore it, and act accordingly.

Professional speakers also have to deal with the unexpected and be ready to think on their feet. For example, you cannot anticipate and prepare for every question that the audience members will ask. And unexpected things will happen, from a power failure to a fire alarm to someone in the audience needing medical assistance.

A few years ago, while waiting to present a session on "Thinking on Your Toes" to an audience of fifty people at a client's company, I was stung by a wasp on the back of my leg. Because this was the first time I had ever been stung by anything, I didn't know what kind of response my body would have. My mind instantly envisioned the worst case scenario: I could have a severe allergic reaction and go into shock in front of the audience.

Luckily, an in-house emergency medical technician gave me first aid and declared that I showed no signs of a severe allergic reaction. So I went ahead with the program and shared the wasp story with the audience, using my ice pack as a prop and relating the experience to my presentation. The audience appreciated the humorous and practical, though accidental, example.

Despite your best plans and preparation, sometimes things happen at a speaking engagement that you cannot control. In that moment when the unexpected happens, move forward spontaneously. Be calm and trust yourself.

RULE #2: STEP OUT OF YOUR COMFORT ZONE.

I had never acted on stage in high school or college. I started taking improv classes as an adult because I thought it would be fun. Several of us from class, including a few people I knew from local Toastmasters International® clubs, started meeting to practice improv comedy for fun and as a way to improve our speaking skills. At that point in my evolution as a speaker, I was memorizing my speeches, so the thought of going on stage without a memorized script or even an outline was far outside of my comfort zone.

Over time, we formed a cohesive team of eight people and began performing in 2004, first for a Toastmasters club and then at the local library for a few friends. The small shows and many hours of practice led to shows at Gotham City Improv in the ultimate comedy location—New York City.

Returning to the opening scene at Gotham—I was that person who had to become a spelunker one of the first few times I stepped onto Gotham's stage—the scene bombed. We adjusted the lights on our hardhats and admired the stalactites and stalagmites, though we weren't quite sure what they were.

We never established who we were or where the caves were. The scene had no energy, and we got very few laughs. We had taken a risk and moved outside of our comfort zone—and failed. But we used the failure to help ourselves grow. We watched the video, got feedback, analyzed what went wrong, and worked on improving our skills.

"Stepping out of your comfort zone" has several applications for speakers. You might get in a rut after speaking for several years on the same topic. After getting good at delivering your signature story, you may get bored with it and just phone it in. Stepping out of your comfort zone can help revitalize your content and delivery. Even small changes can help. For example, approach your topic from a different viewpoint. Or if you usually tell a story all in your own voice, tell it in the voices of the characters.

Stepping out of your comfort zone takes thought, preparation, and practice. It's a risk, and sometimes you will bomb, as I did in the spelunking scene. But that measured risk can have a big payoff. Trying something new can be fun, propel you forward, and make you more engaging. It helps to focus you in the moment, forces you to grow, and allows you to learn from your mistakes.

RULE #3: KEEP IT SHORT.

Improv scenes last only three to five minutes. In that short time, the actors have to figure out and communicate who they are, where they are, and what they are doing—and be funny. You have no time for elaborate setup or extraneous information. When the director yells, "End scene," your time is up.

Professional speakers are used to working with a much longer time frame, but that does not guarantee success. Some speakers rush through their material, go over the time limit, and then look surprised when they have to be pulled off stage. Even if you don't make the mistake of going over the time limit, being more focused and succinct within the time limit improves your presentation.

An improv exercise, "Half-Life," helps people learn how to cut extra material so they can deliver their message within the time limit. In this exercise, two people improvise a scene in 64 seconds, based on a suggestion of a location from the audience. Then the actors repeat the same scene in half the time, 32 seconds. Rather than just talking faster, they have to cut out the extra material in the scene and focus on the essential elements. Then they perform the same scene in 16 seconds and then in 8 seconds and sometimes, even in 4 seconds. When the timer starts beeping, the scene is over.

You can apply this technique to your speeches. Once you've developed a general outline for a speech, "half-life" it by cutting out the extra material so you can focus on the essential elements of your message without going over the time limit. It helps you create a focused speech where every anecdote, statistic, and example clearly relates to the central message.

RULE #4: ADVANCE THE SCENE.

When you're in an improv comedy scene, the goal is to move the scene forward and prevent it from stagnating. One technique, "Yes And," advances the scene by requiring you to accept whatever information or idea the other person on stage has offered without denying it or negating what he or she has said.

You can also advance the scene by building in emotions like happiness, sadness, anger, and fear. Instead of just talking about the emotions, you show them to the audience nonverbally. You can also add object work, which consists of your interaction with pretend physical objects (not real props) that fill your space. For example, you can open a taxi door, sweep the floor with a broom, or take pictures with a digital camera.

Variety also advances the scene. You can change either the stage picture (how you're using the physical space on stage) or the tempo. If you've been moving quickly and throwing out lines at a fast pace, then suddenly slow down. Variety makes the scene interesting and keeps the audience's attention.

All of these techniques for advancing the scene have clear applications to the world of professional speaking. "Yes And" can help reshape how you think about audience questions or comments from other speakers on a panel. It doesn't mean you have to agree with every wacky or off-base remark. It means you treat others' ideas with respect and try to build on them.

You can also add emotion to your stories and use your nonverbal communication to make the emotions more evident. In the case of object work, you can use real objects as props (though that does require practice to be effective) to help the audience remember the message. Varying the stage picture or tempo can capture the audience's attention and highlight the important parts of your speech.

RULE #5: DON'T TAKE YOURSELF TOO SERIOUSLY.

During improv comedy shows, I've had to slither on the ground like a snake, dance like Michael Jackson, and save the world from a giant marshmallow in my role as the superhero "Big Hair Woman." I cannot take myself too seriously after those experiences.

So how does this apply to speaking? Take your craft seriously and work on it, but don't take yourself so seriously. Confidence comes from being yourself—your best self—without being cocky. As your best self, be nice to people around you, including your fellow speakers, the audiovisual staff at speaking venues, and potential clients.

Earlier in my career, I was scheduled to speak at a national conference in a concurrent session along with several other speakers. Technicians worked in a flurry of activity before the session to make sure they set up the stage correctly for each of us. One speaker looked overwhelmed and dashed around trying to get ready, but when I offered to help, she snapped at me. She treated the hotel staff poorly and dealt with a microphone problem as if it were a catastrophe and a personal insult. She created such a sense of negativity around her that when she delivered a speech on personal development, no wonder it turned out to be mediocre.

Be mindful of your stress levels. Accept the fact that speaking does have a lot of moving parts to manage, and things will never go perfectly. If you find yourself overly stressed and negative all the time, remember why you got into the speaking business. Reconnect with your purpose, and if you're no longer able to achieve it without taking yourself too seriously, then perhaps it's time to make a change.

These five rules of improv comedy help foster creativity and build a shared, original experience with the audience. If you apply these rules to your work as a professional speaker, you can unleash your creative energy and build a powerful connection with the audience. In that moment, your speech brings together a unique blend of your knowledge, skills, and experience, enhanced by the audience's background, perspective, and needs, and delivered using your mind, heart, and body.

The house lights dim, the audience waits expectedly—and you take charge. "Begin scene!"

Gilda Bonanno is a speaker, trainer, and coach who helps people improve their presentation and communication skills so they can be more successful. She achieves these results by combining her extensive business experience with a talent for improvisational performance and a belief that, with the right training and practice, anyone can become a more effective communicator. She has worked with clients throughout North America and in Europe, China, and India. Gilda is also a founding member of the World Class Indifference improv comedy team, which performs shows and conducts workshops in New York City and Connecticut. She incorporates improv techniques into her speaking, training, and coaching, helping people learn to think on their toes, be creative, and develop confidence. She is president-elect of NSA-CT. Visit www.gildabonanno.com.

COOKING UP COMEDY

Molly Cox, Dale Irvin CSP, CPAE, Bill Stainton,
and Ron Culberson, MSW, CSP

Much like a master chef's culinary creation, fresh and high-quality ingredients make the difference in a recipe for humor success. So, where do you find those grade-A ingredients to make your speeches funnier? We do not have PhDs in humor. What we offer is comedy club, mainstage NSA, Second City, and The Brave New Workshop experience. Also, parenthood and hospice. We've traveled from Boise to Beijing, and so far (fingers crossed), we haven't had to send any checks back.

We ask ourselves daily, "Is the ability to be funny learned or innate?" Probably both.

Delivering great humor requires a tremendous amount of nuance. From dramatic pauses and facial expressions to the punch line, your humor must hit the mark to engage the audience's full attention. And to get good, you must practice.

Mike Sacks, author of *And Here's the Kicker*, said that any book on humor must contain the following statement offered by Mark Twain, "Analyzing humor is like dissecting a frog. Few people are interested, and the frog dies of it." We're not going to tell you why things work, but simply that they do and how to deliver humor on target.

THE INGREDIENTS

So, where do ideas for stories and bits come from? Everywhere. Life—the good, the bad, and the ugly. Gathering comedic anecdotes is like going grocery shopping. The world is a grocery store, and the shelves are stocked with everything you need to mix up a big ole batch of comedy borscht. But just because it's all around you doesn't mean you'll remember it.

That's why you should get a notebook. Never leave home without a pen and a notebook because you never know when you're going to see something funny and want to remember it. You can also record observations on voice recorders or cell phones. The important thing is to find a device that works for you and make sure you have it with you at all times.

One of the funniest pieces of physical comedy is quite possibly Bill Cosby's dentist routine. It's a must-see to understand the power of facial expressions, the use of space, and timing. But the origin of the bit was something we all do—go to the dentist. After his routine trip to the dentist, Cosby probably took out a notebook and wrote down something like this: *Dentist asked me a question every time he put tools in my mouth.* That one sentence may have been the jumping off point for an entire three-minute scene. And a TV show followed by a multimillion-dollar career. *May have been.* You get the idea.

STOCKING UP

In a grocery store, you stock up on staples like potatoes, rice, and cereal. In the comedy world, your staples are known as *stock lines*. There are a lot of joke books to choose from, and inexperienced speakers think these books are all they need for comedy stew. Well, that's only if you like bland potato-rice-cereal stew. Or lutefisk. Use stock jokes sparingly. The best approach is to make sure it's uniquely yours. For instance, a bland joke would start, "Two guys walk into a bar . . ." while a more interesting version might begin, "My uncle Binky and I went into TGIFriday's . . . on a Tuesday . . . because uncle Binky is weird like that . . ."

USING FRESH INGREDIENTS

Incorporating current events—even better, those that are localized—are audience favorites that help show off both your wit and your intelligence. Before you speak, research the local news in the city you're speaking. Find out what stories have the greatest relevance for the audience. Make your comedy as personal as possible, and keep it fresh.

Some of the freshest humor is ad-libbed. An ad-lib or improvisation is a last-minute decision that can make or break the program. Like Tabasco sauce, it can add the perfect kick, but it could also ruin the meal.

Watch the pros. Quickness, plus wit, plus timing makes the perfect ad-lib. Jon Stewart—good at ad-libs. Al Gore—not so much. One of the best ad-libs came from Ronald Reagan, CPAE. After the attempt on his life, he was taken to the hospital with a gunshot wound. As the doctors were preparing to operate, he looked up and said, "Please tell me you're all Republicans."

SWEET SPOT

Dessert is always the best part of a meal. That's why Uncle Binky eats it first. Hey, you know what that was? It was a "call-back." A "call-back" in humor refers to a second (or third or fourth) joke about the same item (Uncle Binky). The "call-back" usually gets a big laugh because the audience recalls the original joke that made them laugh and enjoys the new joke as well.

Congratulations—you now have your ingredients! Now it's time to move to the kitchen and cook up the ideas—transforming these ingredients into comedic material. With the ingredients you've collected, you can either make some appetizers—individual, bite-sized jokes—or a main course—a complete personal story. Let's start with the appetizers.

APPETIZERS

The most interesting recipes combine two or more different ingredients that don't seem to belong together. The most interesting joke does the same thing: combine two or more ideas that don't seem to belong together into a surprising, satisfying joke. Once you have your raw ingredients (your ideas, your attitude, and your point of view), whipping up a great joke is really a simple, two-step process: 1) setup and 2) punch line. Let's break it down so your joke is neither underdone nor overdone, but just right.

The setup. Just as too many cooks spoil the broth, too many words can spoil a setup, which should be short, containing only the information necessary for your audience to "get" the punch line. Keep it simple. Ideally, the most crucial ingredient—the word or idea that is the key to the punch line—should be at the end of your story.

The punch line. When we're talking about humor, we're not talking about formulaic jokes; we're really talking about stories. The most important thing you need to know is that a great punch line, like an expertly applied dash of spice, should *punch*. Virtually all great punch lines have a punch *word*. This is the word (or, in some cases, a phrase) that forms the surprising, satisfying connection between the disparate ideas. If you really want to add some sizzle to your jokes, make the punch word the last word in your joke. Example: *Take my wife, please*—funny. *Please, take my wife*—not funny.

MAIN COURSE

Every great chef has a signature recipe. Every great speaker has a signature story.

Come up with a humorous premise from your life. Ask yourself: When did something go wrong? This is where your comic vision comes in. The wedding stories, the vacation stories. Nobody wants to hear about your perfect vacation; they do want to hear about your lost luggage and how you had to wear someone else's underwear for two days.

As you write your story, begin with a structure. One of the oldest—and still one of the best—is the three-act structure, which includes simply a beginning, middle, and end.

Beginning. The beginning of your story gives the basic information or foundation your audience needs to understand the rest of the story—and ultimately, get the punch line.

But it has one other, crucial ingredient: a goal. The protagonist of the story (generally you) has something he or she wants to achieve. This must be established in the beginning. Tip: The more important the goal (at least in the protagonist's mind), the funnier it is when things start to go wrong.

The beginning is often followed by the "Oh @#$% Moment." Your transition from the beginning of your story to the middle happens when the first thing goes wrong. Example: Your beginning establishes that you're running late to pick up your spouse to get to a very important dinner (say, to meet the in-laws). You run to the car—and you've locked the keys inside. Congratulations—things have started to go wrong.

Middle. The three-act structure has been described this way: 1) Get your hero up a tree. 2) Throw rocks at him. 3) Get him down. The middle is when you throw rocks at him. You add more humor by adding more conflicts to the situation. Anytime the protagonist overcomes one obstacle, he or she is hit with something else. This is the fun part!

End. Resolve the story. What happened? Did the protagonist (let's assume it's you) achieve his or her goal? What did you learn? Now tie it to the point you're making in your speech, and you've given your audience a great meal.

For a great example of this structure, listen to Grady Jim Robinson's drum major story. His daddy was the football coach, so when Grady was old enough to play, his daddy told him to go down and get his cleats for the football team. After several stalls, he sheepishly told his daddy, "I don't think I want to be on the football team. I want to be with the band." His daddy asked, "Do you play an instrument?" to which he replied, "No, I'm going to be the drum major." At this point Grady channeled his father, took a long drag on a cigarette and asked, "Where ya gonna live?" Brilliant, interesting, and satisfying. The key is originality.

YOU EAT WITH YOUR EYES FIRST.

When setting the table for humor, remember the three senses of a successful laugh banquet: verbal, visual, and experiential. As a humorist, you need to know how to combine these senses according to your unique abilities and your personality. As Amy Sedaris expertly tells us in her book, *Hospitality Under the Influence*, "Every person is special. In all the land, there is only one of you. Possibly two, but seldom more than sixteen."

Verbal Humor

We're speakers; words are our stock and trade; we convey humor through quotes, jokes, and stories. Verbal humor will sustain most audiences for the length of any program if properly presented.

Formulaic jokes are a frequent offering of novice speakers. While formulaic jokes can certainly get a laugh, you can do better. The Internet gives us easy access to jokes, puns, and one-liners. What will make you sparkle is originality.

One exception to that originality rule is incorporating quotes, which when used sparingly, strategically, and with proper attribution, not only support your presentation, but position you as a well-trained humor expert. When accepting the Mark Twain award for humor, Steve Martin pulled a piece of paper from his pocket and said, "This evening reminds me of one of my favorite Mark Twain quotes. I wrote it down so I wouldn't forget it. 'Whatever you do, don't name an award after me.'" A wonderfully positioned quote—even though it was made up!

Stories

Your own recipes are the best. A humorous personal story, just like mom's Thanksgiving stuffing, has flavor and texture that is unique to the creator. Look for opportunities to incorporate your stories strategically throughout your program. Here's an exercise to get you started:

For the next five days, pay attention to the little things that happen to you. Or things that happen to other people.

Stuck at the airport? What happens?

Your washing machine bubbles over. What happened?

Talked about your mother-in-law to your wife while in your baby's room—didn't know she had the other end of the monitor? What happened?

All of these events could make really funny stories. They're like a newly picked carrot. The center is good, but it must be washed and peeled.

Visual Humor

Verbal humor does not stand alone; it often needs a visual to carry it to its full potential. That's your expression and occasionally props. Visual humor complements and enhances. How entertaining would a ventriloquist be if you heard it blindfolded?

Most often, visual humor does not stand alone, but some talented humorists can pull it off. Take, for instance, Tim Gard's starfish story. In a performance called "A Night of a Thousand Starfish," twelve humorists in the National Speakers Association retold the classic starfish story à la The Aristocrats. In other words, each humorist used a different method of telling the story about a person throwing starfish back into the sea to prove that small actions can make a difference. It was an amazing event with absolutely no duplications—even though the performers had not consulted with one another. Creativity was at its finest that night. Two of the humorists used visuals—in this case, costumes—to enhance their stories.

Tim Gard had a custom-made silk-ish starfish costume that extended the length of his arms, legs, and two feet above his head. The costume was not only hilarious, it inhibited Tim's movement. He barely made it onstage and then could not bend over to pick up pages of his script that blew off of the music stand. Instead of being embarrassed and stumbling over his lines, Tim, the consummate professional, milked the visual humor for all it was worth. The audience was in hysterics as he attempted to reach for his script without success. Additionally, his first-person narrative of the story made for a unique angle as well.

Molly Cox was carried onto the stage in a mermaid outfit. She was draped over two chairs and she reclined with a cigarette in her hand as if she was the underwater version of Mae West. Her fin flopped over the chair arm. As she told the story using cheap detective novel language, the costume and her carefully chosen words, paired with hilarious facial expressions, created a uproarious experience for the audience.

Consider using funny visual aids to spice up dull slides or handout materials. Like salt and pepper, a well-positioned photograph, cartoon, or video will add depth to any recipe.

Experiential Humor

We save the best for last. Family-style restaurants leverage the joy of sharing. Similarly, interactive humor through games, interviews, small group discussions, and improvisation allows the audience to enhance your humor with their own ingredients for an unexpected and spontaneous delight. Consider involving them in your next creation.

For a good example on how to do this, watch almost anything Steve Spangler, CSP, CPAE, does on Ellen DeGeneres's show. At the 2009 NSA convention, Steve involved us all in an experiment. He had provided every person with a windbag. He instructed us all to try to blow and blow and blow, counting the number of breaths it takes to get it full. Then he showed us how, by opening the bag and blowing one big breath, it would pull other air in the bag (Bernoulli's effect). While he was teaching us, we were all laughing, connecting, and truly part of his presentation. One caveat: If you are not skilled at using ingredients with a high probability of an impending explosion, you might want a different mentor. Someone like Bob Pike, CSP, CPAE, a master of interaction. To date his presentations are very interactive and have few audience injuries.

If all of this were easy, everyone would do it well. But great humor delivery is a valuable commodity. Scarcity determines value. That said, it's easy to do.

Steve Martin's arrow-through-his-head bit was funny because, well, he's Steve Martin. The key to delivering great humor is knowing yourself. Steep yourself in what works for you. Like a good cup of Darjeeling on a cold night in Juneau. If the tea bag sits in hot water for the perfect length of time, it's good. Not funny, but good.

The thing is, we can't make you funny. We can make you look funny. We can make you smell funny. But hey, you want to make a living. The danger of too much analytical thought destroys the essence of the fun, so if anytime it's too hard, back off and try a different direction. Make sure you have the right ingredients, and put yourself in the right atmosphere for creative thought.

For us, a check and a deadline usually work best to get the juices flowing.

Bon Appétit.

Molly Cox is the coauthor of *Improvise This! How to Think on Your Feet so You Don't Fall on Your Face*, twice on the CEO READ top 25 list. Molly helps people find more laughter and joy in everything they do, resulting in higher productivity and greater personal happiness. She recently produced the film, *Note to Self: An Inspiring Film for Caregivers*. www.mollyspeaks.com www.NotetoSelfthefilm.com

Ronald P. Culberson, MSW, CSP, is Director of Everything! at FUNsulting, etc. and Head Writer at Funnier Speeches, LLC. He is the author of *Is Your Glass Laugh Full? Some Thoughts on Seeing the Humor in Life* and *My Kneecap Seems Too Loose: 365 Random Thoughts to Inspire Deeply Shallow Thinking*. A former hospice social worker and senior manager, Ron helps organizations achieve a new level of excellence through humor. He shows people how to have more fun while maintaining the integrity of the work they do.

Dale Irvin, CSP, CPAE, is the author of eight books and is the world's only Professional Summarizer, constructing up-to-the-minute comedy commentary for conferences and conventions. His goal is to make meetings more fun because when people have fun, they learn more. Subscribe to Dale's "Friday Funnies" for free at www.daleirvin.com.

Bill Stainton is a multiple Emmy Award–winning television producer, writer, and performer. He is the author of *The 5 Best Decisions the Beatles Ever Made—A Handbook for 'Top of the Charts' Success*, and coauthor of *Humor Us: America's Funniest*

Humorists on the Power of Laughter. He blends the business smarts he learned from twenty years in corporate management with the show biz sparks he gleaned from working with people like Jerry Seinfeld, Ellen DeGeneres, and Jay Leno to create entertaining and enlightening presentations enjoyed by audiences around the world. Visit www.OvationConsulting.com

MOVE YOUR AUDIENCE WITH THE RIGHT BODY LANGUAGE

Patti Wood, MA, CSP

When you speak, what does your body language say to your audience? The latest research says that people form an accurate first impression (measured 80 percent accurate or higher) in as little as one three-hundredths of a second. You may spend weeks or months perfecting the content for your presentation, but communication research shows that much of the audience's impression of you, as well as its attention and emotional response to you and your message, is determined by your nonverbal behavior.

How should you present nonverbally? There are always things to learn whether you are a beginning or seasoned speaker. You may want to take a video of your latest speech and watch it, and then take notes as you read this chapter.

1. THE POWERFUL START

The first thing you say or do in front of your audience has the most power to grab its attention or lose it. Most researchers agree that doing something that is novel or unique, rather than what is expected or "normal" for a speaking situation, will gain the most attention. Nonverbally, that can be anything from jumping up and down, doing cartwheels, speaking very loudly, running from the back of the room, or simply not standing front and center with your arms at your sides or behind a podium. Do something different with your body and voice to start.

Step forward.

The most "honest" part of the body is from the waist down. It is under the least conscious control and tends to be the first part of the body to respond under stress with a freeze, flight, or right response. It is not surprising for speakers under stress to freeze or step or lean back in retreat. To show power and confidence, step forward. My favorite trick is to have speakers step toward the audience as they begin their speech, when they ask for questions, and when they close their presentations, or any time they may feel they are losing the audience.

Watch your stance and posture.

It may seem elementary to say stand with your weight evenly distributed on both feet. But when you are balanced center, you actually appear more balanced to the audience. Power is communicated by taking up space. To look strong and feel strong and confident, the ideal stance is to stand with your feet six inches apart for women and six to eight inches apart for men. If you place your feet farther apart than that, you risk appearing defensive and/or aggressive to your audience. In fact, men will typically broaden their stance to twelve inches or more when they begin to debate or argue, so, guys, watch your feet during Q and A.

Small nonverbal changes affect how audiences view us. In the first televised U.S. presidential debates, candidate Richard Nixon severely bumped his knee getting out of the limo to enter the debate. He stood behind the podium, favoring one leg, looking oddly *crooked* to the television audience. In a poll of television viewers, Nixon lost by a landslide. In the poll of those who only listened to the debates on the radio, Nixon won by a landslide.

In the Kerry-Bush debates, Bush more often had a broad stance and more relaxed overall body language, while Kerry's was smaller, and he often leaned to the side. When running for president, Barack Obama had a larger stance, stood up more straight, and maintained a more open posture than any of the Democratic or Republican candidates.

2. FACING THE AUDIENCE

Face toward the audience and give them your heart. Audiences see an open posture and view you as confident. The limbic brain reads it as, "This guy is not guarding himself against attack."

When you face your heart toward your audience, instead of toward your notes, your laptop, or your screen, you are also symbolically letting them know they are the most important element in the room. You're showing that you care about them.

Before you begin your presentation in a training setting, you may need to work on your equipment or notes, but turn and say hello to people as they enter. And try to finish your setup quickly, so you can actually stand by the door and greet people as they enter. It seems like a small thing, but sharing your heart by connecting with your audience before you begin speaking has a powerful impact.

3. MOVEMENT, ROOM, AND SPACE

For some of you, movement is basic, but it is so important to get out from behind tables, podiums, and other barriers. Use the room—control your space. Take over, go out into the audience. Research suggests that if you move in the first few moments of a presentation, your audience gives you permission to break the third wall later in the presentation. Another bonus is that breaking the third wall and moving out into the audience has been shown to increase attention and decrease bad behavior, including side conversations, cell phone calls, and texting.

Walk around the stage, auditorium, training room, or boardroom table. You do not need to stand still in the center of the room for the entire speech. More than ever, you need to move, move, and move some more to hold attention and energize the audience. *In fact, your body's movement actually helps the audience feel like they are moving so they are less fatigued by sitting still and listening. Your movement should be purposeful, rather than pacing. Stand in place, and then make a point and move. Do this when you make each point or tell another story.*

4. FACIAL EXPRESSIONS AND BODY MOVEMENT

The speaker smiles, runs across the stage, and says with enthusiasm, "I am so excited to be here today." That is magical. However, one of the dangers of giving a speech over and over is that you might act the speech, rather than *feeling* it.

When I read interrogation videos for law enforcement and the media as a deception-detection expert, I look for the natural synchronous nonverbal cues that show honesty. We feel an emotion, then we show it with our bodies and facial expressions, and then we say it with our words. For example, we naturally smile before we say, "I am having a great time." And grimace before we say, "I am mad."

The time between each action may be only a millisecond, but for those listening and watching a speaker, a change in that order is unsettling enough to affect the central nervous system. When someone is lying, the awkward and unnatural timing happens when he or she is thinking, "Here is the planned content (or lie). I will say it. Pause. Now, I have to think of what I should feel about that. Pause. OK, now I should smile and gesture this way."

The nonverbal cues come late. Speakers should make sure they express themselves in the naturally synchronous way. When a speaker is acting rather than feeling what he or she is saying in the moment, the beat is off. The presenter may speak before he or she feels. When you're speaking, always focus on your feelings first.

5. HAND GESTURES

Psychological scientist Spencer Kelly from Colgate University and Asli Özyürek and Eric Maris from Radboud University Nijmegen (the Netherlands) were interested in the interaction between speech and gesturing, and discovered that gesturing helps audiences learn the material more effectively if the gestures match the words. In fact, other research shows that when a speaker's gestures and words differ, the audience will process the meaning of the gesture rather than the word.

Consider this example: A speaker plays Simon Says with his audience and says, "Put your hand on your chin." But as he speaks, he puts his hand on his nose. The audience members will put their hands on their noses. Your gestures are powerful.

When I coach speakers on improving their body language, I hear: "What do I do with my hands?" The hands come out from the heart, and symbolically reveal true feelings. Nervousness and anxiety flow from feet and hands. We don't want our fear to show, so we want to hide our hands. Most of the frustration comes at the beginning of the speech when you are the most nervous. You may want to plan specific gestures to use at that time. I throw my hands up in the air at the beginning of one of my speeches just to get the excitement up and out of my body.

The location of your hands also affects your nonverbal behavior. Put your hands at your sides and your energy goes down; your voice lowers and can become more monotone; and you tend to move less and show fewer facial expressions. Bring your hands to the level of your waist and you become calm and centered. Bring your hands up high to the level of your upper chest or above, and your voice goes up and you become more energized and animated. Change the location of your hands depending on your emotional message.

If gestures are an issue for you, take the time to create an opening movement. Whether it's waving "come on" or making a funny posture with your hands on your hips like Superman, Wonder Woman, or Iron Man. Or if that is way out of your comfort zone, and you are extremely nervous, merely plan to start with one hand in your pocket and magically the other hand will gesture.

Have you ever known people who "talk" with their hands? There are more than 100,000 possible hand signals using different combinations of postures and arm, wrist, and finger movements. Gestures serve all sorts of communicative functions. They link and support our words. Gestures can add meaning, demonstrate we are listening, punctuate sentences, illustrate a point, give additional information, and more.

Research, such as that by Dalbyetal (1980), says lecturers make twice as many hand gestures as people who are talking one-on-one. Rather than reduce your gestures when you're having trouble remembering your speech, you should increase them, because research shows that gesturing accesses more neural pathways in the brain and creates more connections, thus smoothing out speech and reducing pauses and vocal utterances such as "uh."

As a professional speaker, I'm aware that gestures help me form my messages. When I was just starting my speaking career, I remember one night after a week on the road when my body and mind were especially tired. It was 10:30 p.m. when I began an after-dinner speech. I very consciously increased my animation and gestures, and within seconds, I felt energized. The funny lines came out smoothly and effortlessly, where just a moment before I was struggling. Move around the room and gesture to help you speak smoothly and effortlessly. It works like magic.

Right Hand . . . Good. Left Hand . . . Bad?

Does it matter to you and your audience which hand you gesture with? Well, in laboratory tests, "right- and left-handers associate positive ideas like honesty and intelligence with their dominant side of space and negative ideas with their non-dominant side," says Daniel Casasanto of the Max Planck Institute for Psycholinguistics in Nijmegen, the Netherlands. When examining spontaneous gestures in presidential debates during the 2004 and 2008 elections involving two right-handers (Kerry, Bush) and two left-handers (Obama, McCain) researchers Casasanto and Jasmin found that right-handed candidates made a greater proportion of right-handed gestures when expressing positive ideas and left-handed gestures when expressing negative thoughts. But the opposite was found for the left-handers, who favored their left hand more for the positive and their right hand for the negative.

For years, I have told my public speaking students who were nervous to try putting one hand in their pocket. For 30 years, I have seen students who do this magically gesture with their dominant hand. As a coach for politicians, the old school was to tell them to gesture mostly with their right hand and to use their left hand only when delivering bad news. The new data that Casasanto reports shows that people associate "good things with the side of their body they can use most fluently—dominant is fluent, and fluent is good."

What to Do with Your Hands

- Keep your hands in view, rather than behind your back or in your pockets. When I trained law enforcement officers on interrogation, I taught that one of the key places to look for deception is the palms of the hands. It is very difficult to lie with the palms of your hands exposed.

- Take all change and foreign objects out of your pockets, so you don't sound like Santa's sleigh. If you *must* put one hand in your pocket, one stress-busting trick is to leave a nickel to squeeze.

- Let your gestures flow naturally. They are a reflection of your authentic presence.

- Turn up the volume on your gestures. Practice being more animated, more expansive, more powerful. I'm only five feet tall, yet over the years, most of my audiences are surprised when they approach me after a session and discover that I'm a munchkin.

- When making points, use your fingers to count and hold your spread-out hand high so the audience will know that you are counting for them.

- Be aware of distracting hand motions—rubbing an earring or your mustache, clicking the top of your magic marker, twisting your hands, and pushing back your hair. Lions don't fidget. We often use these gestures while under stress. Watch yourself on videotape, or have someone monitor you—even if you've been speaking for years.

- Diversify your gestures. I've never coached anyone who gestures *too* much, but I've often seen people do one particular motion *too* much. Make delivery changes when hands are below the waist, at the waist, and chest level and higher.

6. EYE CONTACT

Eyes were designed to go toward movement, so we could spy moving game and catch our supper. Now, as speakers, it is obvious, yet so vital, to make eye contact with our audience (often after supper). Maintaining eye contact with an audience is proven to make the speaker appear more skilled, experienced, and powerful. The people we look at are more likely to remember what we've said. Because we take in 80 percent of our information with our eyes, monitoring the audience throughout a presentation is critical. It allows you to connect and be authentic.

- The primary function of eye contact is to establish relationships. Each person in the audience with whom eye contact is established will feel connected to, even befriended by, you, the presenter, and that energy will give you even more confidence. Give the most contact to the person or section who needs it—someone who may be drifting away or talking with a neighbor. We have the tendency to give the most eye contact to the people who are smiling and nodding their head. The "goodie" audience members who are already with you can recharge your energy, but you need to make the most contact with the audience members who are not present in a particular moment and draw them in.

- Looking at, then looking away from, individuals allows us to process and access information. Slowed blinking helps our overall thinking by giving us time to scan our brain for mental pictures and respond to an audience. You don't have to stare at everybody in every moment of your speech. But you do need to look at the audience.

- The end of the speech is the time when most speakers get caught up in the rush to close and forget to be present. Make the most significant, lingering eye contact at the *end* of your speech to create a powerful impact, connection, and closure.

7. MOVEMENT TO SHOW A CHANGE TO A NEW MAJOR POINT

To create the right mix of movement, you can choose to introduce each major point of your speech at a different "station" on the stage or location in the room. You could go to a point in the room, say point number one, from the right front corner, point number two from the left front corner, point number three from the center. You can even return to the points. So go to those points as you preview the points in your introduction, return to each one as you give details and finally go to each point one more time as you review the points in your conclusion.

Our eyes stop noticing what is still. There is the scientific explanation of why you go to sleep when a speaker stands still and drones through his speech! Unless there is a change, the chemical reaction within the rod or cone of the eye comes to a stop, and no further electrical transmission is made to the brain. Hence, the object disappears. Your nerves take about one-twentieth of a second to "reset." So you need to reset your audience's brains by creating purposeful movement.

Patti Wood, MA, CSP, was called "the gold standard of body language experts" by *The Washington Post* and credited in *The New York Times* with bringing the topic into the national consciousness. Patti has degrees with a specialization in nonverbal communication and was a university instructor in body language and other communication topics. She is the author of seven books, including *Success Signals—Understanding Body Language, The Conflict Cure*, and *Easy Speaking—Dynamic Delivery*. Patti is a professional speaker and consultant for Fortune 100 companies. Her clients include AT&T, Hewlett Packard, Proctor and Gamble, Kroger, UPS, Fannie Mae, Porsche, Coca-Cola, and Cisco Systems, as well as hundreds of national associations. She speaks on PBS, the BBC, CNN, *Regis and Kelly*, FOX News, Tru TV, MSMBC, *In Session*, The History Channel, *Inside Edition, The Soup*, The Discovery Channel, and more. She appears regularly in hundreds of print and online media around the world, including *Esquire, Us Weekly, Psychology Today,* MSNBC, *USA Today, The London Times, People,* AOL.com, *Women's Health, In Touch, OK!,* Reuters, *Ladies Home Journal,* ESPN, *Men's Health, Details, Oprah Magazine, Entertainment Weekly, Family Circle, Red Book, Parents Magazine, New York Magazine, The Wall Street Journal,* and *Redbook.*

DRESS FOR SUCCESS

Janice Hurley-Trailor

THE VISUAL IS VITAL.

Before you open your mouth, you have already delivered your first message. Will your audience perceive you as attractive and successful—someone they want to emulate? Your audience wants to look up to you. Does your visual message match the fabulous speech or workshop you have so carefully prepared?

Or will they worry that you struggle with basic life skills?

When you project health, fitness, confidence, and attractiveness, your audience begins to receive your message at first glance. You would never dream of presenting information that is out-of-date or poorly organized, so be sure your personal presence matches your message.

Here are some of the most common mistakes professional speakers make. Could any of these statements be made about you?

1. Your clothes and shoes look tired.
2. Your hairstyle is out-of-date.
3. You look okay from the front, but not so great from the back.
4. You're afraid that looking current will keep people from taking you seriously, so you look boring instead.
5. You haven't changed your clothes to fit your changing physique.
6. You only get into your "speaker's look" just before you go on stage.
7. You haven't figured out how to eat healthily and exercise on the road.

8. You think other people need help with their look but you don't.

Attractiveness might include receiving a few beauty genes from Mom and Dad, but it's far more important to project your magnetic personality and a consistently polished presence. Nothing can replace being well-groomed, but your posture and energy convey that you respect yourself and expect others to do the same. And you send that message from your entrance, to the final applause, to the visual and verbal memories people take home.

THE LONGER YOU'VE BEEN SPEAKING, THE MORE YOU ARE AT RISK.

Some speakers who are early in their careers do a better job of looking stage-ready. Meanwhile, more seasoned speakers can forget how important the visual is, or even stick to styles they saw on successful speakers when they started out many, many, many years ago. For National Speakers Association (NSA) members, the longer you have been in this business, the more interested you are in updating your speaking skills, your marketing materials, your support staff, and your fees. You work brilliantly to keep your message relevant and fresh. Don't let your personal appearance lag behind.

I once helped a seasoned NSA leader choose clothing for his upcoming video shoot. I found that his huge walk-in closet was full, yet he had nothing to wear: Everything was too small, his wardrobe featured old-school pleated pants and suspenders, and the colors did nothing for his skin tone. He looked pale and washed out. It turns out that his beautiful, well-intentioned wife had chosen colors she was drawn to; they looked fabulous on *her*!

We shopped together for updated clothes to fit his physique, in colors to complement his coloring. He gave up his suspenders. And he even lost 25 pounds. He was always a handsome man, but now he looked younger, more fit, and more congruent with his message of power and success.

Getting older in the business, or beginning to speak at an older age, brings great advantages, as long as you update your style. Don't confuse looking *current* with looking *trendy*. Don't look trendy unless that fits your audience and your message. Simply being current will help the younger members in your audience believe that what you're about to say will be relevant to them. Having a well-groomed, flattering, current appearance is essential to gaining your audience's interest and respect.

SO, WHERE DO YOU START?

Invite a friend or colleague over for the day, hand him or her a camera and permission to tell you the truth—and maybe a glass of wine—and get ready for some fun. You'll need a full-length mirror and a sense of humor to get the most out of this emotional experience.

Why emotional? Because cleaning out your closet will force you to confront your beliefs on such touchy subjects as body image, money, and hoarding. It might even challenge a perception you have of yourself that no longer fits.

It can happen to all of us, even me. I swam competitively in high school and college, so I saw myself as having the physique of a swimmer—broad shoulders with tiny waist and hips—but that was a while ago! As long as I held on to that old body image, I kept clothes that were too tight and unflattering.

Taking current photos of yourself in a bathing suit (front, back, and sideways) should be done in the privacy of your own home. It may not be for the faint of heart, but you are a person with the courage for professional speaking; you can do this.

And now try on the outfit you feel the very best in, and have your friend take photos of that from all sides as well. Analyze it from the standpoint of color and fit, and assess why you like it so much.

Next, clear your closet. Remove everything: all clothing, shoes, and accessories. Try on every item, and with feedback from your trusted friend, sort everything into three piles:

1. Perfect.
2. Alterations. The fabric quality is still good, the style and color are flattering and current, and a small alteration will make it fit perfectly.
3. Goodwill. It's in good condition, but it does nothing for you and never will, no matter how you alter it. Release these to someone who can use them. (If you've kept things that aren't in good condition, add a fourth pile for Trash.)

Men

- Men look fabulous in a crisp white dress shirt and a current tie. If you don't have an ample supply, start there.
- Discard or donate any ties that look tired and frayed, or are too wide—more than 3½ inches.
- Pants should meet the heels of your shoes. If you're standing up straight and they aren't long enough, donate them.

Women

- Give away those jackets or dresses with big shoulder pads. There's one exception: If you are smaller in the shoulders than the hips, you can even out your silhouette with a small shoulder pad. I said *small*!
- Skirts should be hemmed to the middle of your knee or just above.
- When trying on all your shoes, look at your feet and legs from all sides. If a pair doesn't flatter your ankles and legs, give it away.

Putting It Together

Now mix and match items from the first two piles.

Women, separate the matching pants, skirts, and jackets. No more matchy-matchy. Switch those around, wearing jackets over dresses or with different pants and skirts.

Men, you get to match your suits as usual.

Now return only the items from the Perfect pile to your closet and organize them by item and color. Jackets together, pants together, etc., from lightest to darkest in each category.

The average person wears only 70 percent of his or her wardrobe. Beat the odds and be an overachiever. Get rid of what doesn't fit or flatter, and shop for what you need from an informed viewpoint. You'll save money, and you'll command more respect and earn more money on the platform.

YOU DON'T GET TO RELAX JUST BECAUSE YOU'RE NOT SPEAKING.

From the moment you leave your home until you return, you are presenting yourself as a speaking professional, and you're contributing to others' perception of your value. At the airport, and when you arrive at the venue, you attract attention. Plus, oftentimes, the meeting planner who hired you has never seen you before, and looking the part of a professional, well-paid speaker helps you start on the right foot.

Maybe you're speaking at a weeklong conference where your part is only an hour. You might be tempted to be lax in your professional attire before and after the day you speak, but that would be a huge mistake. Other meeting planners are often in attendance, and you are making a lasting impression on them and on your audience. Whenever you attend a conference longer than your stage time, look the part consistently. Once you have spoken and established your credibility, you might feel less pressure to look stage-ready, but now everyone recognizes you; it is even more imperative to look polished and professional. Pack accordingly, and prepare to garner repeat and spin-off engagements from each presentation.

TAKE CASUAL SERIOUSLY.

Often, we are expected to attend casual events or outings associated with a conference, and it's a great perk to meet people and enjoy the scenery. Take the time to choose appropriate attire for each event. It can be more challenging to pull off a professional casual look than to create your stage look. Casual time does not mean sloppy. Make a point to be pressed and polished, even when casual.

When I work with speakers, I often find they have skipped whole categories in their wardrobe. They have nothing appropriate for casual events or formal evening events either. Prepare for both settings so your presence is consistent, creating the optimal perception of your talents and value in every setting.

Men, unless you are on an actual beach in Hawaii, I don't recommend the classic beach shirt. A crisp button-down shirt with rolled-up sleeves can be just as weather appropriate, while creating a more confident, successful presence. And avoid showing your feet in sandals. It's rarely appropriate for you, especially if you haven't had a recent pedicure.

Women, avoid showing too much skin. Please, no cleavage, no flip-flops, and nothing short enough to bring all attention to your legs. Even in casual attire, create a professional appearance and draw attention to your face. If your arms are still attractive and firm enough, you can wear sleeveless, but a partial sleeve is always worth considering for a more professional look.

TRAVEL WITH PURPOSE.

Have you ever booked a speaking engagement because you met someone on a flight or in transit? If not, why not? While traveling to large conventions, you can easily find yourself sitting next to someone with connections who could hire you for a similar event. Just as you perfected your thirty-second elevator speech, prepare your image as carefully. Everything about you, from your luggage to your shoes to your business card, should say, "I am a well-paid professional speaker" or "I am a well-paid expert."

Many emerging NSA members or candidates are holding another job as they launch their full-time speaking careers. You'll be more confident and willing to introduce yourself as a professional speaker when you know you look the part, and you will be treated accordingly. When I tell people what I do, my favorite response is, "Of course! You look the part!"

Speakers will say they dress down because they want to be comfortable when they travel. Hallelujah! No question about it. I promise you—you can do both. It takes more thought to find comfortable professional shoes, and create a traveling wardrobe that works, but it is doable. Traveling like a pro ensures you look the part as you arrive, and as you meet people from all walks of life along the way.

So, how many other speeches will you book from your travel encounters? Make it a goal to welcome and attract those opportunities every time.

LOOK LIKE YOUR MARKETING MATERIALS.

Check your marketing materials—your photos, your videos, your online presence, your business cards, your one-sheets—and make sure everything accurately, consistently, and realistically represents what your audience will see. It's tempting to alter our photos beyond recognition, because we can! I'm right there with you, wanting to remove the crow's-feet or trim a sagging jowl line, but don't do it. A great photographer employs flattering lighting, but don't enhance your picture so much that people don't have that immediate recognition when they meet you. Keeping your image consistent means updating your materials often, or keeping your present look consistent—your call.

And remember to treat your fellow NSA members as well as you treat your target audiences. When members see how committed you are when they meet you at chapter meetings and NSA conventions, your membership investment and exposure will pay off more quickly. Sometimes speakers invited to present to fellow professionals show up looking less than stage-ready, which weakens credibility and suggests a lack of respect. If you're an established celebrity among NSA members, you might not feel the need to follow formalities, but what's the downside of looking sharp? You'll find you feel more comfortable and confident when meeting new members or interacting with old friends, and you'll be more successful in sharing referrals.

IT'S ALL A MIND-SET.

Looking and feeling great are all part of a mind-set, one that is much easier to conjure up with a little homework. Clear that closet, refresh your wardrobe, update your videos and photos, and plan and pack with the clear intention to represent your best self and your message at first glance.

This is a wonderfully rewarding business, and you don't want to miss out on the opportunities and success you desire because you forgot to give this one aspect of your career its due respect. Make it fun, and you'll raise your income. See you on stage!

Janice Hurley-Trailor, The Perception Expert, is a keynote speaker, business consultant, executive coach, and one-on-one image makeover consultant. Janice is based in Scottsdale, Arizona, for her personal makeovers and workshops, and she travels nationally and internationally for speaking and business consulting. She uses the science of body language, verbal skills, and presence to achieve optimal results for her clients. Janice knows that successful people aren't successful by accident. They have learned how to have a compelling presence, and Janice shows her clients how they, too, can achieve that. For more information, visit www.janicehurleytrailor.com.

FROM BACKSTAGE TO ONSTAGE: PREPARE TO SHINE!

Kevin E. O'Connor, CSP, and Cyndi Maxey, CSP

Backstage can be a lonely place. Even when you're surrounded by your audience, as many speakers are in the moments before they present, those moments are solitary moments. Actors have a dressing room followed by a greenroom and finally a dark, off-stage space to prepare. Speakers, on the other hand, are often among the crowd, or at best, next in the line-up on a noisy, shallow stage at a corporate meeting. While most speakers prepare their presentations, their slides, and their anticipated interactions in advance, it is vital for speakers to prepare for the *moments before* the first word is spoken. Just like an actor, a speaker needs a "backstage" in which to prepare—whether that "backstage" is in the audience, the hallway, or the mind.

Here are a few ways some speakers spend the moments leading up to their presentations. They might sound familiar.

- Hanging out in the restroom for a quiet place to calm the nerves.
- Avoiding listening to the previous speakers for fear of a break in concentration.
- Staying at the front of the room and double-checking the projector, computer, and microphone, and reviewing notes.
- Checking the phone for e-mails one last time.
- Blocking out everything but awareness of the present.
- Off to the side of the stage, rehearsing the opening line over and over again.

- Pacing the hallway, letting go of negative energy, and building upon adrenaline's positive influence.

These *moments before* are critical for both the experienced and beginning speaker alike because they do two things: They set the speaker's inner tone, and then they help shape the outer message conveyed to audiences. You will discover that some of these techniques are healthy and work to a speaker's advantage; others are less so. How about you? What do you do just prior to your first words? What goes through your mind 30 minutes prior? 15 minutes to go? 5, 4, 3 . . . ? As you are introduced?

These moments are critical because you aren't just addressing friends and fans. All speakers address three audiences simultaneously: 1) those who are eager to hear, 2) those who are watching and deciding whether to hear, and 3) the speaker's inner self-confidence. Each is a vital audience that warrants attention.

- **The audience that is ready to hear.** Those who came to hear are rooting for you. They want to hear what you have to say, and they are readying themselves for your first few moments. They want to say "yes"; they want to nod with approval; they want to be right in their decision to come.

  But be careful not to assume too much here. While you may have a great reputation, a best-selling book, or celebrity status, you must still earn the respect of your audience. Communicate with them—not to them. Communicating "with" is considered horizontal communication, which puts you on an even plane. When you speak "to" them, you run the risk of being perceived as feeling superior to them, and few today are willing to tolerate being talked down to. When you do so, they may not stand up and leave, but they certainly won't listen, nor will they like the experience—or you—very much. This group is on your side at the start, but it's up to you to keep them there.

- **Those who are deciding.** Just prior to your speech, there are those who will size you up, using nonverbal cues to decide if you are a worthwhile use of their time. This does not mean they are skeptical or critical; they are simply using their most readily available sense—what they see. Let them see you. Don't hide behind the audience or a curtain. If possible, be accessible, available, and authentically you. Unless you are quite famous or are speaking in Madison Square Garden, engage the audience visually during your introduction. It's often their first impression of you at a time when they are looking for a sense of your confidence, your ego, your humor, and your overall personality. Let the positives shine through. This is the time to ensure that your facial expression exudes a healthy blend of charisma and credibility.

- **Your inner self-confidence.** No matter how often you have given this speech, you must realize that you need to create the same positive mindset each time. Regardless of any disturbing phone calls the night before, a recent cancellation, a lingering e-mail, or an ill parent, you are "on" to present to this audience, at this time, in this place. Your confidence must expand beyond the material; it must reflect your entire self. When you bring your whole self to the moments just before approaching the platform, you are truly present.

  How can you rev up your inner self-confidence? The best way is to align your thoughts along a mental mantra such as: "I'm happy to be here," "I love what I do," "Focus on them," or "This is for them, not me."

For all three audiences, there is one important first task for the speaker—connection. Watch how others connect and even how some fail to do so. When you watch your pastor or rabbi connect with you each week, observe what he or she is doing. Does he quote scripture by heart? Does she gesture to illustrate opening concepts? Does he smile before he begins? Does she poke fun at herself right away? Likewise, what happens when you watch a newsmaker who goes right to the point?

And when you sit in on the speech just ahead of you (always do this!), position yourself to watch the audience and note what sparks their connection with the speaker as you listen to the speaker.

All three audiences will give you continuous feedback. When you don't listen to the feedback or fail to understand the importance of the three audiences, you run the risk of appearing:

- Distracted. To the audience, this looks as if you are unprepared.
- Not fully present. To the audience, this appears to be just another show.
- Not engaging. This makes an audience feel unimportant.
- Not connected. This creates unnecessary distance with the audience.

- Dependent on the audience's first overt reaction, laughter, or applause. This puts you at great risk of a flop opening.

- Unprepared. This is the ultimate insult to an audience.

So, what can a speaker do in the moments before? These five things will help ensure a fast connection with the audience:

- **Meet the audience.** Nothing will give you a better opportunity for a warm and receptive audience than greeting audience members as they come in, sit down in their seats, or stand in the coffee line. You will notice a spike in your evaluations, a more responsive audience, and smiles right from the beginning. Why? Because you are making individual connections before you have to rely on your opening words to connect with the entire group. Audience members typically enjoy meeting the speaker in advance. Bring your best extroverted self to the table. Say hello, shake hands, thank them for coming, and just enjoy them. Try to meet all of them person-to-person—or in larger audiences, aim for 20 percent, and the rest will notice you are working the crowd and will feel a part of your effort.

- **Enjoy the introduction and make eye contact.** Your introduction should begin your dialogue with the audience. Situate yourself so the audience can see you off to the side of the introducer. This way, they can see you listening and reacting to your introduction. Remember, the introduction is not a biography, a resume, or a marketing tool. It is a "handshake" with the audience to let them know who you are, what they have in common with you, and what you have to offer them. Humor in the introduction will help your introducer engage them and make your audience laugh (your first way to connect and engage them). Then when they see you enjoying the intro, you will appear human and safe to them. You can help them to like you immediately.

- **Connect with yourself and remember your past successes**. In the moments before, remind yourself of your strengths as you have known them in the past. This audience will somewhat resemble those past audiences and also be somewhat different. Tune into your strength of content, of flexibility, and of focus. This focus helps you stay aware of the important things that happen for individuals who are unknown to the speaker. This is the time to repeat your "mental mantra" and really believe in it!

- **Use your first two minutes wisely.** Your first words, your first story, your first slide should serve only one purpose: to help the audience confirm you are worth listening to. Throw something substantial to the audience for them to chew on rather than the mundane details of your flight, the city, a joke, or a profuse thanking of this or that person. You can do all of that later. Right now you must engage. When you thank or comment on the meeting or city, the audience is not listening to you. This generic approach signals your own nervousness and is an amateur way to start your speech. When you let them know early and firmly that you are worth listening to, you will experience no trouble from then on. A poor opening is difficult to recover from and difficult for the audience to forget.

- **Practice your opening story with a real person—better yet, with many people.** Humorists and comedians are always practicing. They test new material amid old material they already know generates laughs. They experiment. We can do the same. If you have a story you think is a great opener, find a way to fit it into your normal day-to-day conversation with others and then watch their reactions. Change it up here and there; notice your timing, and closely watch their reactions along the way. On your way to the talk, tell the story (out loud) to yourself in the car with many variations. Now you won't sound as if you memorized it because you'll have many iterations of the story. They will sound spontaneous because they are!

Finally, remember that "just prior" you should be a bit nervous. You should wonder what's in store. And you should be ready to take the next right step. Energetic. Curious. Courageous. These are the characteristics of the pro who uses his or her backstage time well.

Kevin E. O'Connor, CSP, and Cyndi Maxey, CSP, are veteran speakers and facilitators. They have coauthored the books *Present Like A Pro: A Field Guide to the Art of Business, Professional and Public Speaking* and *Speak Up: A Woman's Guide to Presenting Like A Pro*, both published by St. Martin's Press. Kevin can be reached at (847)208-8840 (kevin@kevinoc.com) and Cyndi can be reached at (773) 551-9599 (cmaxey@cyndimaxey.com).

TOP TEN BIGGEST CHALLENGES PROFESSIONAL SPEAKERS FACE TODAY

Nido R. Qubein, CSP, CPAE

Just when you think you have your act together, life changes and you start facing a whole new set of challenges.

Some challenges are temporary and require only minor shifts in thought and action. Yet, all too often, the new challenges run so deep and are so permanent that they demand a whole new set of strategies to survive and prosper in the speaking business.

The following ten questions focus on the major challenges that all professional speakers face and some strategies to cope with them:

1. ARE YOU AN UNCLEAR REACTOR OR A CLEAR PRO-ACTOR?

Are you an unclear reactor? No, that's not a typo. An unclear reactor is a person who is so unclear about what's going to happen that he only reacts after it happens.

An unclear reactor likes to *go with the flow*, to take things as they come, and to keep life in the present tense.

Unclear reactors are content to get big-name ad agencies to design pretty brochures for them, to jockey their fees up and down to fight competition, and to face each day with no clear-cut direction.

For example, speakers who are unclear reactors will take any booking that comes along without regard to whether it fits their area of expertise, their schedule or the image they are trying to build. To them, paradise is doing 300 engagements a year.

The problem is that unclear reactors soon burn out, or they get so scattered that no one (not even themselves) knows who they are or what they do, or they spend all their time dealing with crises. They simply react to what happens.

In contrast, the clear pro-actors take charge of their own lives and careers. They set goals—both personally and professionally. They develop solid strategies and invest all their energies to make the right things happen.

Check your own patterns by the following ways of expressing either reactive or pro-active responses:

Unclear Reactors Say	Clear Pro-actors Say
We've got a problem!	We have a challenge!
People want too much!	How can we give more value?
I want more money!	How can I meet more needs?
If it feels good, do it!	If it fits the plan, do it!
Let's do something,	Let's make sure that what
even if it's wrong!	we do is right!

Experience shows that over the long haul, it's the clear pro-actors who always lead the pack.

2. ARE YOUR STRATEGIES FRAGMENTED OR INTEGRATED?

"A camel is a horse put together by a committee," someone once said. This is a reminder of the way many new professional speakers put together their strategies. They develop random strategies that don't support each other or move in any clear direction.

Even good strategies will not get the job done unless those strategies are integrated into a whole plan that accomplishes your overall goals.

For instance, recording a CD or writing a book because *there's a market for it* is fragmented thinking. A poorly conceived and executed product that fails to properly position your services can be like a millstone tied around your neck. You might make a few bucks on it, but its ultimate cost in lost opportunities could cost a fortune; it might even derail your career.

Real success in this business comes from multiplying your efforts in every conceivable way through a systematic strategy of applied consistency. That begins with structuring your engagements in a way that fulfills your objectives and is strengthened by having products, proprietary components, and cooperative ventures that completely fit with your career objectives.

3. ARE YOU ON A MISSION OR GUIDED BY VISION?

Many speakers build their careers through a series of isolated missions, with no overriding vision of guidance. Unfortunately, just when they are on the brink of breaking through to some real success, they burn out or become disillusioned with their missions.

It is one thing to blindly commit to a cause you believe in and, like Don Quixote tilting at windmills, throw yourself into that cause. When that happens, it's easy for your perceptions of reality to be so colored by the mission that you fail to see things as they really are.

It is, however, far more productive to have a guiding purpose and the clarity of vision that enables you to see the big picture and to know where you fit into it.

4. SURE, YOU KNOW HOW, BUT DO YOU KNOW WHEN?

Knowing how to give a good performance, how to promote your services, and how to hit the market with new products is vital to your success. What many people fail to realize is that knowing when and with whom to do all those things is sometimes even more crucial.

In this business, timing is everything.

For example, when you've done a great job on a speech and the top brass of the sponsoring organization showers you with compliments, the tendency is to gloat. You might think it's a good idea to follow up and try to get more business from that account at some future date.

What I've learned is that the best time to sell more of my services is when people have just expressed happiness with what I've done for them. I will move in right then to pin down a date for the next meeting, or to set up needs analysis sessions, or to sell my consulting services.

That way I'm building on my success and not trying to make something happen after the fact. Besides, experience has taught me to take advantage of every opportunity to talk to decision makers. Sometimes, it's the only chance we have to reach them—and it's the easiest way to make contact.

5. DO YOU MERELY THINK ABOUT IDEAS, PROBLEMS, AND OPPORTUNITIES, OR DO YOU THINK THEM THROUGH?

Most of us can come up with more ideas and have more opportunities than we could ever cash in on. And we all face more problems than we could ever hope to handle.

Because there are so many things hitting us from so many directions, it's easy to fall into a pattern of merely thinking about things, rather than really thinking them through. To do that is like looking at the visible tip of an iceberg and believing we see the whole thing.

Thinking things through involves projecting the long-term impact of every action, weighing the impact of that action on every facet of your career, and creating strategies to deal with all reasonably expected contingencies.

As you plan, for example, think of three things that can go wrong with your plan and develop ways to deal with them. If you can't think of three things, something is unrealistic.

Or, when a bright new idea hits you like a bolt out of the blue, think it through clearly enough to make certain of its viability—before you act on it.

6. ARE YOU MANGLED BY YOUR LOAD, OR DO YOU MANAGE YOUR LOAD?

When engagements are a little slow to come, it's easy to think that being over-booked would be a nice problem. But it's amazing how quickly and completely your workload can take charge of you, rather than vice versa.

Pacing yourself so that you can enjoy your life and always be at your best may prove to be one of the toughest challenges you will face as a professional speaker.

It's tempting to say that the more successful you become, the bigger the challenge. However, the reverse more often is true—the better job you do of pacing yourself, the more successful you will become.

For instance, you need to sell for the slow times during the busiest peak times.

If you don't allow enough time to sell when you are at your busiest, and if you don't sell services for your off-peak times, your careers will constantly rise and fall like roller coasters.

You can't always sell a keynote position or just your sales seminar. You must sell wisely—to sell enough to keep busy, at a pace you can maintain over the long haul.

Another key to managing your load is to focus on billable hours. A major key to success in this business is not just staying busy, but always doing something you can logically bill to one of your clients. Otherwise, you become your own greatest overhead expense.

7. DO YOU KNOW HOW TO BALANCE COST AGAINST VALUE?

The cost of a product or service is what you must charge the client to recover expenses and make it profitable. But it is the buyer who always sets the value.

That makes pricing one of the trickiest parts of the speaking business. If you price a product or service too high, the clients won't buy. But if you underprice, you can lose your shirt.

Oddly enough, many products don't sell well because they are priced too low. Why? Because most people seem to feel that "you get what you pay for."

I recently negotiated a major training contract with a large banking institution in which my price was several times the price quoted by my nearest competitor. What made the difference? The client was convinced that my action plan was a great value—even at several times the price of my competitor.

I've found that the greatest tactic in pricing is to price my services and products high enough that I cover all my costs (including taxes and hidden costs) and make a reasonable profit, and then build mountains of value in presenting it to the prospective clients.

8. DO YOU LIVE BY FALSE ECONOMY OR MAINTAIN FISCAL STABILITY?

It's easy to busy yourself with the wrong things and believe you are incredibly successful. It's also easy to find one thing that works well, and one client who will keep you busy most of the time, then focus on that one activity and client.

Another thing that's easy is to get large advance payments from several clients, spend it all on current expenses, and then get caught with more time commitments than you can fulfill. This especially is problematic when you commit yourself for several years at a time.

All those practices are formulas for disaster. They lull you into a false sense of financial security that can create tremendous pressures for you and your staff.

Ideally, no client should have more than 20 percent of your time, and no single activity should ever eat up more than 25 percent of your schedule. Otherwise, if a client withdraws or an activity quits selling, you suddenly can find yourself starting over.

Fiscal responsibility certainly includes monitoring and controlling expenditures, but it is equally concerned with allocating resources. Good fiscal planning includes: providing the resources you need to accomplish your goals, prioritizing your expenditures of time and money, and allotting enough time to complete all the projects you start.

9. CAN YOU MARKET AND SELL EQUALLY WELL?

Marketing is a term that describes the total activity of delivering your services and products to all the potential customers who would buy them. It runs the full scope of activities from conceptualizing, research, and development, to advertising, selling, and handling distribution.

Selling, on the other hand, is concerned with actually building value, handling objections, and closing sales with one customer at a time. It's what most salespeople call *getting the order*.

If you were part of a large corporation, you'd probably be concerned with only one minute part of the total marketing and selling effort. But most speakers have to wear all the hats and fulfill all the functions of marketing and selling.

Of the two functions—marketing and selling—selling is by far more crucial. It's this simple: If you can't get people to actually purchase your products and services, the most elaborate and costly marketing/advertising/promoting plan won't do you any good.

The most important advice I could give to a novice speaker is: "Learn how to sell!"

Take a look at your own track record and ask yourself how well you sell. If you are not satisfied with your answer, invest whatever time and resources it takes for you to learn to sell. The better you can sell, the more successful you will be in this business.

But once you master the selling process, move on to become equally competent in marketing.

10. ARE YOU FIGHTING FOR SURVIVAL OR LIVING IN PERPETUAL REVIVAL?

It is one thing to survive; it is quite another to keep yourself from suffering burnout.

When you find yourself on the road, hitting the rubber chicken circuit, and always hurrying to make appointments—for months on end—it's easy to lose sight of why you're doing it all.

That's why it is so crucial to stay in touch with your own purpose in life, to take time to invest in vital relationships, and to constantly renew yourself mentally, physically, and spiritually.

It also helps to develop new material and presentation techniques. If you don't constantly grow in your performances, your enthusiasm will eventually get weaker and weaker. It won't be long before your audiences will notice the difference and you'll be forced to slow down for the wrong reasons.

The only way to maintain your standards of professionalism over the long haul is to build in a system of constant personal renewal and professional revival.

THE CHALLENGE OF THE CHALLENGE

One thing that makes this business so exciting is that each day brings a host of new challenges. As you rise up to meet those challenges with hope and courage, your life can be continuously enriched.

That's what growth is all about. It's struggling against tough odds, stretching to new stature, and reaching for new heights. It's never easy, but it can always be fun.

Nido R. Qubein, CSP, CPAE, is an international speaker and accomplished author on sales, communication and leadership. He is president of High Point University, which has an enrollment of more than 3,500 undergraduate and graduate students. Nido serves on several national and local boards and is the recipient of numerous awards. He is chairman of Great Harvest Bread Company, with 218 stores in 42 states. For more information, visit www.nidoqubein.com and www.highpoint.edu.

SEVEN KEYS TO GET UP, GET SPEAKING, AND GET PAID

David Newman

Economic cycles come and go. Even when the conventional wisdom seems to be that "no one's hiring speakers," you can be sure there's always a bull market somewhere. When it's time to reboot, recover, and reignite your speaking business, these seven key strategies and best practices are indispensable.

KEY #1: PROFESSIONAL SPEAKER IS A SKILL SET, NOT A JOB DESCRIPTION.

What would the average speaker do if he could no longer speak? What if she were unable to travel? For someone self-defined purely as a "speaker," that might be the end of the road.

But they'd still have a professional speaker skill set; it would simply need to be deployed in other ways. With that in mind, it makes sense to get comfortable with those other ways right now. Multiple revenue streams provide business-model resilience—when one part of the business is down, another might be up. It's insurance at the very simplest level. Building that insurance into the speaker's business plan today ensures getting paid for expertise regardless of industry trends, personal challenges, or unexpected family issues.

Best Practice #1: Diversify methods and media.

Consider:

- Books

- E-books
- Workbooks
- Field guides
- Meeting starters
- Audio programs (CD, mp3, podcast)
- Video programs (DVD, streaming, mini-lessons)
- E-learning modules (using simple tools like Articulate Presenter)
- Consulting packages
- Coaching programs
- Teleseminars
- Webinars
- Action packs
- Implementation kits
- E-mail courses
- Membership websites
- Online forums and communities
- Assessments
- Mobile apps
- Certification programs
- Licensing programs
- Affiliate programs
- Joint ventures

Choose the most suitable methods, get them on the calendar within the next year, and execute!

KEY #2: EVERY SPEAKING BUSINESS NEEDS A CEO.

The primary trait that separates successful speakers from their struggling counterparts? *Successful speakers don't consider themselves speakers.* They consider themselves the CEO of their speaking business. CEOs demand a relentless focus on MMA—Money-Making Activity. CEOs know when their company is profitable and when it is not. CEOs have the rare skill of being able to panic early—and then taking massive, decisive action to correct the course before it's too late.

Most important, CEOs are never OK with *not* making money. They put all their weight, all their creativity, and all their commitment behind making payroll. Speakers who think they don't have employees are dead wrong—they're Employee #1. Are they paying themselves enough? Do they give themselves enough time off? A CEO would give priority to the employee responsible for 100% of her company's profitability. A solo entrepreneur speaker needs to do the same.

Best Practice #2: Schedule paydays.

Speakers who have employees already have a payroll. But a company of one needs to do the same, just without payroll software or vendor—even if it's a simple as marking the calendar for the second and fourth Friday of each month as "payday." The quickest way to earn $50,000 as a speaker is to divide that number by 24 ($2,083.33) and every payday, transfer that amount from a business account to a personal one. (That's also the quickest route to $100,000, $200,000, or more!) To start, it's easiest to ignore marketing, taxes, operations, and so on, but that's rarely the biggest challenge. The idea is to establish an early warning system that's focused on MMAs when the coffers are running low. The self-paycheck practice provides that, while establishing a much-needed sense of urgency with regard to cash flow.

KEY #3: ESTABLISH A "NOW MORE THAN EVER" MIND-SET.

Too many speakers complain that the economy has damaged their businesses. Buyers are no longer buying. Meetings are no longer meeting. There's a laundry list of aches, pains, symptoms, and woe-is-me declarations of how life suddenly got very unfair for professional speakers.

Three words of wisdom: *Figure it out.*

That means figuring out what buyers are deeply concerned about, what problems they are eager to solve, and what priorities they're already spending money on. It requires determining the strategies and goals for which they are accountable. And it demands ferreting out what solutions they're actively seeking right now.

The speaker who does that is like a doctor during a time of epidemic disease, equipped with the medicine and ready with the cure. In tough times, the services of a doctor are in greater demand, not less. A resource primed to cure a buyer's exact woes will experience limited resistance. So, too, speakers who believe that their ideas are needed now more than ever and are in demand now more than ever will be valued by their clients now more than ever.

Best Practice #3: Live in the prospects' world.

Business-minded speakers think about their clients' problems, bosses, obstacles, and customers—not just their own. What are the first steps? Research. Preparation. Homework. Industry, regional, and company news is now at everyone's fingertips online. Direct quotes, video clips, and audio interviews make excellent firsthand intelligence—and don't forget real, live customers. Without intelligently researching a prospect's issues, challenges, and pressures, it's impossible to come up with credible, high-perceived-value solutions. The most convincing way to approach prospects is being armed with:

- Interviews
- Surveys
- Research
- Data gathering

Expertise plus valuable data is a killer combination.

KEY #4: GET SERIOUS, GET HELP, OR GET OUT.

The top professionals in any field realize that they cannot achieve success alone. They ask for help. They invest in the resources, tools, technology, and people who can accelerate both their learning curve and their doing curve.

What's the best place to start? The good news is that it doesn't cost a dime—it's an internal commitment to take this business of speaking seriously. It's not a part-time thing for fun, it's not volunteer work, and it's not something to "try" between jobs. Do military fighter pilots "try" flying combat missions? Do doctors go into neurosurgery "part-time"? Do symphony orchestra conductors "give it a shot"? No! True professionals make serious commitments to their professional training, years-long preparation and study, thousands of hours of practice, and a relentless pursuit of excellence.

Upon ruthless, objective examination, the areas where a speaker needs help will become quite clear. And that's OK: Successful professionals reach out for help *more often* than average people—not less.

The third option is to get out. This doesn't mean quitting the speaking business—far from it. Rather, it's about taking a professional break and coming back into this business through a different door, which is precisely what I did in 2007. My speaking and consulting business had become a grind. I wasn't having fun. I needed a break. I took a job at a training company, booking speakers for events, webinars, and live conferences.

Within two weeks of wearing my conference producer/meeting planner hat, I immediately realized what I had been doing wrong as a speaker. In 2008, I jumped back into my own business, and the lessons from my time "on the other side of the desk" gave me everything I needed to reinvent my speaking business and share these same lessons with my professional speaker clients on what it takes to get booked from the buyer's perspective.

Best Practice #4: Recommit.

Getting serious means recommitting to the speaking business: upgrading collateral materials; losing the dated aol.com email address; dumping the homemade inkjet business cards; and revamping that 10-year-old website.

Getting help might include: free help (NSA buddies, colleagues, friends, mastermind groups); low-cost help (NSA chapter meetings, webinars, PEGs, hiring an assistant or intern); premium help (attending an NSA convention, working with a speech coach, hiring a speaker marketing firm).

Finally, getting out can vary from the moderate to the extreme. Consider a part-time consulting or on-demand position with a favorite client, association, or company to see what makes them tick. Do some subcontracting or get a job with a training company, consulting firm, or executive education program. Speaker's bureaus and conference-producing organizations are also terrific options. Don't consider this as exile; it's a paid learning experience. Keeping one's identity as a professional speaker helps, too: While I was working on the inside, my business card proudly displayed the NSA Member logo right next to my title.

KEY #5: BUILD A THOUGHT LEADERSHIP PLATFORM.

A speaker's collected body of wisdom, expertise, tools, tactics, strategies, sound bites, and philosophies compose a thought leadership platform. New technologies and new media come and go. Consider the evolution from print newsletters and glossy magalogs through websites, e-zines, blogging, audio, video, and social media—but the one thing that does not change is professional speakers' need to be thought leaders.

Writing is writing. Ideas are ideas. It may sound like heresy, but if Ben Franklin were alive today, he would be a blogger, thanks to the technology's ability to reach a great number of people quickly with ideas that positively impact their lives.

Best Practice #5: Repurpose.

The sound bite is "Create content daily." Meeting planners want to see a speaker's thinking process, showcased in meaty articles with lots of specifics and do-it-now tactics. The key isn't just telling people what to think but, rather, what to do and how to do it. Actionable information is a powerful tool.

Here's a one-word shortcut to great articles: repurpose. Keynotes become articles; articles become special reports; special reports can become audio programs; audio programs can become the rough draft for a book. With a solid thought leadership platform, the different ways to package and profit from ideas are limitless.

KEY #6: BECOME AN NSA CERTIFIED SPEAKING PROFESSIONAL.

Ordinarily, I couldn't care less about industry acronyms. But consider it from the perspective of association executives, meeting planners, and corporate decision makers: If only 8 percent of speakers have a CSP designation and 92 percent don't, who are they going to feel more confident about hiring? It is a risk-reduction strategy for your buyers, an instant recognition of a speaker's professional qualifications.

Yes, there are plenty of exceptional speakers who are not CSPs. But from a buyer's perspective, how many CSPs are likely to be awful speakers whom they will regret hiring? Extremely few. The safer bet gets booked more often.

Best Practice #6: Get certified.

Start an application at www.nsaspeaker.org. The CSP tracking spreadsheet and application packet make it simple to record stats rather than trying to reconstruct the who, what, where, and when five years down the road.

KEY #7: FOCUS MARKETING ON THE MIGHTY FEW.

The era of "better, faster, more" productivity is over. Multitasking is a myth, and good luck "getting things done." The sad truth is that most professional speakers catch the disease of *tacticitis*. They believe they have to listen to the guru of the moment and belong to the coach-of-the-month club, while simultaneously working on their presentation skills, marketing, branding, website, video, book writing, sponsorships, social media, list building, article publishing, and networking. (And that's before they try to regrow a full head of hair and lose those unwanted pounds.)

Best Practice #7: Focus on business-building strategies.

The latest guru, offer, product, program, and technology that lands in your inbox has less to do with succeeding than does having a solid business model, speaking model, and revenue model—and they're usually a lot more expensive. It's far better to select two or three main strategies that can be used consistently. Writers should write. Techies should use technology. People persons should network.

The truth is, the "flavor of the month" rarely lasts a full year. In contrast, working harder on fewer things, and focusing exclusively on easy, effortless, and enjoyable business-building activities, is what will yield results—this month, next month, next year, and for the foreseeable future. The marketing geniuses at Nike have had it right for a long time: *Just do it!*

David Newman is a marketing speaker and founder of Do It! Marketing, a marketing strategy and "done-for-you" services firm dedicated to making professional speakers successful. David serves as 2010-2011 president of NSA Philadelphia, and was named Member of the Year in 2009. Check out his 97-page *Strategic Marketing* e-book at www.doitmarketing.com.

SIMPLY THE BEST!
CREATE A COMPELLING AND
AUTHENTIC BRAND FOR YOUR
SPEAKING ENTERPRISE

Dick Bruso

Sam can't wait to get up in the morning to share his passion and expertise with the marketplace. His compelling and innovative brand aligns perfectly with who he is, as well as his niche market. He's great at what he does.

Contrast this with Susan, who quite candidly admits she's lost her passion for speaking and stands at a major crossroads in her career. She's doing well from a financial standpoint, but she increasingly believes what she offers the marketplace doesn't represent who she really is and her unique take on things.

So, if they're both successful, what's the true difference between Susan and Sam? In my experience, the best branded and most successful speakers have three key traits in common:

- They know who they are and, as a result, do what they love.
- They fully embrace their niche markets and expertise.
- They are truly innovative in what they offer and how they approach the marketplace.

KNOW WHO YOU ARE.

Branding is about focusing on who you are rather than what you do. Your core values, talents, gifts, abilities, interests, and passions ultimately form the foundation of your brand.

To tap into that, you need to ask yourself a tough series of questions—and answer them honestly:

- What values were instilled in you as a child, and what did you excel at?
- If you went to college, did you major in your passion or did you follow a different path?
- What was your first career, and what led you to become a professional speaker?
- Is speaking your primary focus, or does it complement activities such as writing, coaching, and consulting?
- What's your greatest skill? Problem solving? Inspiring others? Serving as a contrarian voice to tackle misconceptions?

When you do what you love and live out your brand authentically, you will, more than likely, generate a powerful demand for your brand.

EMBRACE NICHE MARKETS & EXPERTISE.

Most speakers like to think their messages are universal, but there's significant value in identifying the audiences who can benefit *most*. Niches can be found by position, profession, organization type and topic, or factors such as age, sex, or geographical location. Considered on another level, what kind of individuals do you want to interact with for the rest of your life?

Expertise is the flip side of the niche coin. Overnight successes are rare in the speaking business—the top practitioners offer a depth of experience and knowledge earning them the right to call themselves experts. Whether it's "paying your dues" or "doing your homework," becoming truly knowledgeable about a specific area of expertise is an essential component of a prosperous speaking career.

BE TRULY INNOVATIVE.

There's a major difference between being noise in the marketplace and creating your own unique space. Cirque du Soleil is a perfect example. They took elements of Broadway, combined them with the most exciting attributes of the circus, and created an experience unparalleled in entertainment today. They have no real competition—because they dominate the market they created!

Innovation is an essential element in bringing any brand to the marketplace. In addition to the speaking engagement itself, it involves overall marketing, interaction with clients, and promotion, as well as following up afterward. For many speakers, it also involves the creation of innovative, brand-specific products and services. Any of these points of differentiation need to strive for the truly original, transformational, and remarkable experience—and, therefore, emotional engagement with the audience.

The best comment I've ever heard about a speaker's presentation was, "You had to be there. It was an unbelievable experience and really impacted my life!" Isn't that a piece of feedback every speaker would like to receive? Innovation is an essential step in the process.

A FEW CASE STUDIES: COMPELLING AND AUTHENTIC BRANDS

The Entrepreneur

Steve Lishansky, a successful speaker, consultant and past president of National Speakers Association–New England, refers to himself as a serial entrepreneur, having started and run companies since he was a young boy. Even after nearly 20 years of speaking to and consulting with leaders in 40 countries around the world, he still makes ongoing course corrections to enhance his brand message.

Steve recognized that the name of his firm—Lishansky Partners—did little to convey the benefit of what he had to offer the marketplace. Steve's niche focus is working with the most senior executives and their teams in an organization, as well as high-potential future leaders. His clients are primarily corporate, although he has done some significant business with governmental agencies and non-profits.

Rebranding as Optimize International (of which he's the chief executive optimizer) in 2008 was an ideal solution. "All of my existing clients would tell their friends and colleagues, 'You really need to talk to this guy,' but they weren't able to adequately express what I do," Steve says. "The concept of Optimize has been received with great enthusiasm by every one of my clients. Now they can make the kinds of appropriate and effective referrals that work to expand my practice. They were excited to be able to convey my brand message easily and simply and tell their friends and colleagues that I can optimize their ability to be more effective, productive, fulfilled, and successful."

The Keynoter/Trainer

Sandy Geroux, past president of National Speakers Association–Central Florida, is a former salesperson and award-winning real estate producer. She became a professional speaker, trainer, and consultant in 2001, when she formed The Geroux Performance Group. Initially, she focused her efforts primarily on the real estate industry.

Then, in 2005, she made the transition to helping various corporations and associations significantly improve their relationships in the workplace—but she wasn't gaining any real traction in the marketplace. As a gifted speaker, singer, and entertainer, she also wanted her brand to reflect her effervescent personality. Upon deeper examination, it was clear Sandy was all about creating a "Wow!" experience, which eventually led to the coining of "WOWPlace International: Turning Your Workplace Into a WOWplace."

Today, Sandy's audiences consist of corporate, association, and governmental leaders, managers, supervisors, and their teams, as well as HR professionals—and her brand is totally congruent with who she is and what she wants to accomplish in life. "Changing my brand transformed my business and opened up entire new markets across industries for me—even into the government sector," she says. "The tagline 'Turning Your Workplace Into a WOWplace' grabs everyone's attention as soon as they hear it, and really expresses what I'm all about."

The Emerging Speaker

Kris Harty entered the world of professional speaking on a part-time basis in 2003, and in 2010, she became a full-time speaker and consultant. Her story is one of tenacity and can-do spirit.

At the age of seven, Kris was diagnosed with juvenile rheumatoid arthritis. "It was one of the worst, and best, things that ever happened to me," she says. "I'm a survivor of the 'can't' model.' I was told I'd never learn to drive, attend high school or college, work full-time, live independently, have my own house, or be a successful entrepreneur. To the amazement of my doctors, I've done all of that, and more."

Going into the business full-time required rethinking her branding. Kris's new company name, Strong Spirit Unlimited, testifies to her indomitable spirit, while the tagline "Stick to it—no matter what!" was inspired by her walking stick. In fact, it's more than a slogan; it's her ultimate challenge to her audiences. Her message of perseverance is especially relevant right now to her key niches in the healthcare industry, corporate leadership, sales professionals, and nonprofit professionals.

"Creating a new speaker and company identity formed the very foundation of my business," she says. "It solidified, laid the groundwork, and provided direction for everything I do as an inspirational speaker. I now share my life's wisdom with those professionals who pull at my heart, in an effort to ease the weight of their work and to decrease the cost of fatigue to their employers."

Steve, Sandy, and Kris are exceptional examples of the power of a dynamic brand presence. They know who they are, have a genuine expertise, and have set themselves apart in the marketplace. It's a path every speaker needs to follow.

A RENEWED PASSION

The beginning of this chapter dealt with the challenges a woman named Susan was facing in her speaking career. That anecdote wasn't the end of her story, however.

Susan's steps were simple but powerful. She took a long, hard look at who she is. She has embraced her favorite niche markets and refocused her expertise to align with them. She aims to make every presentation truly innovative and captivating. And, after rebranding her business and rededicating herself to the speaking profession, she is now following her heart, telling her story, and speaking to those audiences she relates to the most.

Dick Bruso, international speaker and founder of Heard Above The Noise®, is a highly regarded branding and marketing expert. He has worked one-on-one with hundreds of professional speakers, authors, entrepreneurs, and business leaders to create and implement powerful branding, marketing, media, and relationship building strategies. Using the dynamic "Umbrella Brand" approach, Dick shows his audiences and clients how to develop and expand their brands to powerfully penetrate the marketplace. He also is an award-winning producer of both traditional and new media projects. Dick is an active member of the National Speakers Association (NSA) and the Global Speakers Federation and a past president of NSA/Colorado. You can reach him at dickbruso@heardabove.com or visit his website at www.heardabove.com.

MONETIZE YOUR MESSAGE: TURN YOUR PRESENTATIONS INTO ADDITIONAL INCOME

Kim Clausen

As a speaker, you have a great message to share. You are a master at your craft, delivering great value, educating, informing, and inspiring others, and impacting lives for the better. But you want more. You want to take your message beyond the podium and create additional income opportunities by developing and marketing supplemental products, services, and training programs.

What if you could extend your income stream beyond the podium? Instead of being on the treadmill of having to find speaking engagement after speaking engagement, what if you could have a thriving business that reaches more people, offers more products and services, and provides you more income?

This chapter is about taking a fresh approach to growing your speaking business using the philosophies and principles of the most successful companies. Five simple strategies that you can easily get your arms around are all it takes to build a thriving multiple-income-stream business.

The essential strategies are based on the acronym TANCS—Target, Attract, Nurture, Convert, and Serve. And implementing all five strategies using education-based communications, products, and services can attract prospects, nurture relationships, and convert more clients.

T—TARGET

The key to expanding your speaking business into other areas of service is to identify a target market that has a need you can serve.

Choosing a target market has many benefits. Simply stated, it allows you to focus your efforts so you can be more effective in your product development and marketing. It is too overwhelming a task to try to reach a general market with general products and messaging, but most speakers can get their arms around the idea of targeting a certain demographic of people who have specific needs they can serve.

By selecting a target market, you are better able to:

- identify where to find your prospects and how best to communicate with them;
- provide more targeted messaging so that you get noticed among all the noise;
- become known in the industry;
- become a credible source; and
- speak more specifically to your target market's needs.

With today's media bombardment and information overload, it is harder than ever to get noticed. General messages to general audiences are sure to get lost in the noise. Targeted messages to a targeted audience have a much higher likelihood of being seen and noticed.

It doesn't matter how great your products and services are if you cannot get them out to your market. And the best way to attract attention, establish familiarity, build credibility, and get clients is to focus your efforts toward one specific population of people.

A—ATTRACT

Once you identify a target market, the next step is to develop strategies to get known in that market. To compete with the multitude of other messages and voices in the marketplace, the best way to attract your prospects' attention is to speak to them about their most relevant needs and interests.

Most of us are in a relationship-based business, and our clients want to do business with people they know, like, and trust. Therefore, we must go out to our market not to sell, but instead to first form relationships. And the only way we can effectively create relationships is to be in continuous communication that is meaningful and relevant.

One of the most effective ways to reach your market, build familiarity and trust, and attract prospects is by providing education-based communications, which put your knowledge and information in the form of how-tos, tips, strategies, tools, and resources that solve a problem or enhance life. When used for attracting your target market, they are usually delivered for free or a low fee as articles, white papers, e-books, teleseminars, webinars, and online audios and videos.

Education-based products and services are the best way to attract your market because they provide value and are not "salesy." And early in the relationship, your prospects do not want to be sold to; they want to check you out and get to know you before engaging with you further.

The good news for you when it comes to creating education-based communications is that you already have a message, a specialty, and an expertise. In other words, you already have content to create your products. In fact, you probably have more content than you know what to do with, and that is why you are reading this chapter—you want to make money with all the knowledge and information you have at your disposal.

N—NURTURE

To nurture is to persistently and consistently make meaningful contact with your prospects once they are on your list, providing value until they are ready to engage in a client relationship with you.

Value has to be established before your prospect will make a commitment to engage in a business relationship. And it is during the nurture stage that value is conveyed and commitments are made.

This is one of the most crucial steps to building your business and the one where speakers struggle the most. Often speakers get frustrated because they are making the mistake of trying to attract and convert without nurturing first.

This phase is also difficult for many speakers because they wonder, "How do I nurture? What am I going to say? What if it takes a long time? That seems like a lot of work. What if they think I am bothering them or I am too salesy?" That's precisely the reason for education-based communications—they give value and inform, they are welcomed, and therefore do not feel salesy.

Education-based products, on topics that improve people's lives and show them ways to do things better and easier, allow you to touch your prospects in a meaningful way that will be welcomed and anticipated.

Here is an example of how you can turn your message into numerous communications that allow you to stay in touch and deliver value:

Let's say your message is on helping people make permanent lifestyle changes so they can live a life of optimal health and vitality. Your keynote is broken down into three areas:

1. Understanding the importance of taking care of your body and the ramifications if you don't.

2. Changing your perspective from thinking that "healthy living is a sacrifice" to "healthy living feels good" both emotionally and physically.

3. The how-tos of living healthy and feeling good about it.

From this presentation you can create products and services that nurture the prospect by delivering value, such as:

- A five-page special report on "Three Ways to Live Well for Life"

- A one-hour teleseminar on "Three Strategies for Staying Healthy and Happy"

- Three articles on each topic above that you include in your newsletter or send as a gift

- A six-part audio or video miniseries on "Are You Older Than Your Age? How to Live with Energy and Vitality"

As you can see, from just one keynote, numerous products and services can be created. These are just your free and low-fee products, and there is an entire line of products that you can create as part of your paid programs, which will be discussed later in the chapter. Also, imagine all the other wisdom, knowledge, and content that you have at your disposal that will allow you to develop an endless supply of products and services that will serve your market.

The good news for you is that you already have your message and content. All you do is turn that into other forms of communication and use it as ways to attract, nurture, and convert new clients.

C—CONVERT

If you are giving value through education-based communications, you also want to be making offers for your prospect to engage with you further. Your prospect wants to be told how to engage with you next. They want to know what you do, what services you offer, and that you are available for hire. That is why it is important that you are always making an offer when providing your education-based products and services.

Your offers can take many forms, which is to say that conversion doesn't mean you have to be selling a product or service. Conversion can be simply leading your prospect or client to *what's next*. This can be another free service or a paid one. For example, a conversion could lead the prospect from your newsletter to a telecall, or from a telecall to a video training, or from your video training to a request for a consultation.

And remember when you are making offers, some will be ready sooner than others. So, just as with the other steps, make conversion a regular and consistent part of your business activities.

S—SERVE

Service is the delivery of your products, services, and programs in exchange for money. In addition to your speaking income, you also have a variety of paid programs, products, and services.

Going back to the example above, you can create paid products and programs such as:

- A six-part teleseries on each topic above—(intro, three areas, putting it into action, commitments).
- A 16-week structured group with training and education, goal setting, and accountability.
- In-home workbook with audio and a journal.
- One-on-one planning, execution, and accountability coaching.

Your presentations are the core of your business, and also the core of your product and service creation. Your business has a circular flow: Your presentations will lead to the sale of your products and services, and the sale of your products and services will lead to more presentations.

Serving is also about creating your brand. This is where you get known for who you are and what you deliver. You don't have to be the best at what you do, but you have to be professional, and it has to show. Deliver quality products and services, and go above and beyond to make each client's experience with you a positive and rewarding one.

In addition, providing quality products and services leads to loyal clients, more referrals, and a successful business.

BACK TO BASICS

There are many viable strategies for building a successful business. But often, the vast amount of choice leave speakers feeling overwhelmed and too paralyzed to take action. Bring it back to the basics and model the proven, tried-and-true principles of the most successful companies.

Target, Attract, Nurture, Convert, and Serve. It is simple, it is replicable, and it is a science. This simple step-by-step formula can help you achieve observable results. By taking your message and creating a variety of education-based communication, you can reach out to your market, get noticed, attract prospects to you, establish credibility, create goodwill, build familiarity and trust, and grow your business.

TANCS will indeed take the mystery out of marketing and give you a powerful and effective way to expand your speaking business into many other income opportunities.

Here's to your greatest success!

Kim Clausen founded Ready2Go Marketing Solutions as a way to help personal development professionals more easily market their businesses by providing completely developed workshops, teleseminars, speeches, and more that they brand as their own to grow their businesses. Kim is a professionally trained coach who has more than 20 years of marketing and business development experience. She has founded several businesses and has developed a successful coaching practice of her own. To contact Kim, go to www.Ready2GoTrainingSolutions.com, e-mail her at Kim@Ready2GoMarketingSolutions.com, or call her at (303) 465-0454.

POWER PARTNERSHIPS:
WORKING WITH BUREAUS

Holli Catchpole

There are more than 300 speakers bureaus across the country, with close to 450 agents working hard to secure appropriate speakers for their clients. These are powerful marketing and distribution channels for professional speakers looking to grow their businesses.

What is a bureau? It is a booking or sales company that sells the services of multiple speakers. Within the bureau, there is an agent, or in many cases numerous agents, who act on behalf of the speaker and on behalf of the customer to match the ideal speaker with their event. With so many speakers, clients, and agencies in the mix, it is important to be very clear about your area of expertise and what industries you are best suited for, and then determine which bureaus are an ideal match for you. Typically, it is much easier and more effective to focus on a smaller, targeted group of bureaus than attempt to appeal to the masses.

FINDING THE RIGHT BUREAU PARTNERS

In today's tough economic climate, agents—like the speakers they represent—are working harder than ever to produce results. And in most cases, those results are far below normal due to tighter budgets, fewer meetings, and event planners who are savvy in selecting the ideal speaker for their event.

Without a doubt, the Internet has also changed the way the speaking business is conducted, but while search engines provide easy access to speakers, they don't necessarily provide reliable access to tried and true professionals.

A trend appears to be developing as more and more speakers are working with fewer bureaus and many bureaus are streamlining their rosters to reflect the speakers that are ideal fits for their clients. The beauty of a good bureau partner is that they know you, your background, and topics; have seen you live; and can recommend you with confidence. This is comforting to clients and encourages them to learn more. Plus, clients benefit because they can work with one or two trusted advisors rather than thousands of eager speakers.

By partnering with a bureau, you can help build their business as well as your own! Doing some homework to identify your ideal bureaus and developing a connection strategy will reap large rewards. Here's how to make the process a little less daunting:

- Visit the International Association for Speakers Bureaus (IASB) at www.iasbweb.org to view the list of member bureaus and locations. If there is a local bureau in your area, that is a great place to start. Agents love to know about local talent they can recommend to clients coming to town. If you have started communications and have a speaking event close to their office, invite one of the agents to attend as your guest.

- Look for bureaus that match your specialty (Healthcare, Financial Services, Agriculture, Sports, Under $5K, etc.), but keep in mind that your client list, content, and marketing copy need to match their specialty. Do not count on the bureau to customize your content to match their target industry.

- Every time you speak, keep a list of the other speakers on the program, and ask your client contact if any of them were booked by a bureau. If the bureau is on your target list, ask your contact if he or she would be willing to reach out to the agent with a reference and recommendation. The agent will pay attention when he learns a speaker was booked without his help.

- As you talk with clients and prospective clients, find out if they have a favorite agent/bureau they like to work with. Calling the agent to let her know her client is also considering you is a valuable marketing investment! It gets an agent's attention and is much more cost effective than mailing $25 media packets and free books to 300-plus bureaus!

MARKETING MATERIALS AND CONTACT STRATEGY

In today's marketplace, we work at a 24/7 pace, and change is constant. As a professional speaker, you need to be constantly looking at the future of our industry and staying on top of the trends and tools that will keep you current. For example, our technology speaker, Scott Klososky, has unique topics and content that is constantly evolving, but a year ago he wasn't being positioned properly. We needed to make sure our bureau partners really knew his background, understood his content, and could recommend him with confidence. So we thought about ways to get the word out.

This challenge came when Twitter was still new and when Amazon had just released the new Kindle. While Twitter was not being fully utilized in the bureau world, it was gaining serious traction. This gave us the idea to host a Kindle contest via Twitter. We selected the agents we wanted to invite to participate, made sure they were set up with Twitter accounts, knew how to use it, and understood the contest rules. The contest lasted four weeks with ten clues (a couple each week). Each clue was announced on Twitter and focused on directing the agent to Scott's bio, topic information, his new preview video, and cool sites they would find interesting. Those who submitted the correct answers to all ten questions were entered into a drawing to win one of three Kindles. We filmed the drawing and posted it on YouTube, so the lucky winners could hear their names being called.

We used a lot of technology components and made it fun and exciting for everyone involved because it was different, it did not require a booking, and a cool prize was involved. The promotion was a success—we exceeded our goal, and everyone eagerly learned something new in the process.

Creativity and timing are crucial if you want to stand out among the thousands of speakers who are doing whatever they can to be recognized. As you look at your marketing materials and contact strategy, here are a couple of tips that might help:

- Keep your website current with constant updates, and make sure it's user-friendly. Speakers are notorious for launching spectacular websites, but then not touching them again for a few years. Visit your site often, and try to view it through the eyes of your bureau partner and target clients. Is everything current and easily accessible at a glance? If you update your site monthly, weekly, or even daily, you are not overdoing it!

Make sure you have unique URLs for each page, so you can quickly send an agent a link to your topic descriptions, testimonials, bio, and other requested information on demand.

- The traditional press kit has gone electronic. The days of sending out packets are thankfully long gone. You'll save a fortune, but the money can be well spent elsewhere—for example, keeping your website current.

- Offer video links. You can be topic-specific and even offer a full-length video to accommodate the varying preferences of agents and planners. It is critical that you have stellar streaming quality. Again, this is an area that needs to be looked at often as technology continues to improve. If the video screen size on your website is smaller than the standard 640 x 480, an update is overdue (and by the time of this printing may already be obsolete). Hi-Def is now available, so seek out any opportunities you can to be recorded using Hi-Def. And if you already have HD footage, use it to WOW your agents and clients.

- Be thoughtful in your e-mail announcements. Keep them customized (mass e-mail is sure to be deleted) and make sure they are newsworthy. Keep your eye out for anything and everything that will help your agent confirm the date. Industry-specific articles or testimonials are helpful, and client references are key. In addition, technology makes it easy to create a customized description, upload a quick YouTube link, offer a Web conference, or do a Skype pre-booking call.

- Constantly watch your calendar for preview opportunities. Again, clients are doing their due diligence, and if your agent can offer their client a local "live preview," it is sure to get their attention even if they can't attend.

MAINTAINING AND BUILDING THE PARTNERSHIP

Once you have your first couple of bureau bookings under your belt, you'll begin to see the momentum build. An outstanding performance will get noticed and talked about. The booking agent will share the news with his fellow agents, who will instantly put you on their radar, too. This is a small industry, and most agents have friends at other bureaus, which gives them the opportunity to share notes and ask for feedback.

An outstanding performance that leads to spin-off business will create an even bigger buzz. Spin-off business refers to any bookings that occur because someone in the audience saw you speak. It is a great way to book more dates and introduce the bureau to a new client.

To leverage one opportunity into another, you need to be uber-focused on tracking where all your leads are coming from. It sounds easy, but when there are multiple players involved, determining the exact source may require some serious detective work. Here are some thoughts to consider as you nail down the best tracking solution:

- Many times the person who calls or sends an e-mail inquiry was not in the room when you spoke, so it is very important to make sure that you (or your team member) ask how they found out about you.

- Associations are prime events for spin-off business because every person in the room is a potential client.

- Before each event, make sure you determine exactly how the agent wants to handle the leads from their initial booking. Not every agent/bureau is the same. Some want the lead the very moment it comes in so they can establish rapport and provide full service. Others want to make sure you have weeded out all the people simply asking for handouts or who just want to exchange business cards.

- Some agencies work by territory, company name, corporations vs. associations, etc., which means the agent who booked you might not be the agent who gets the lead. This is disappointing for the booking agent, but the bureau wins, and it gives you the chance to work with another agent!

- Once you have passed the lead on to the agent, make sure you add the contact to your own system flagged with the booking agent's name. They might call you directly in the future, and this will ensure you know the history and can alert the agent when it happens.

- Most agents are pretty good about keeping you posted on the outcome, but they are focused on their sales efforts, and it is good practice to set yourself a reminder. If you have not heard any updates within a couple of weeks, shoot them an e-mail to check the status. However, it is important to keep in mind how busy they are, so you don't want to overdo it. If they have a hot one in the hopper, you'll be the first to hear about it!

- If there is a lead that comes in and you think it might be a spin-off from a bureau-booked event, but you were unable to determine the exact source, always err on the side of the bureau. This is a good practice, and it helps to have karma on your side.

For a number of years, I have served the NSA/IASB Council, which is composed of IASB members and NSA leaders. Its goal is to enhance speaker/bureau relationships to better serve our mutual clients. The speaking profession is all about relationships, and business partnerships are the key to success. One of the key guidelines is that partnering beats policy every time. For more information, visit www.NSAspeaker.org and access the 2010 Speaker Bureau Relations Booklet.

Holli Catchpole is the president of SpeakersOffice, Inc., the premiere speaker management company for thought leaders and top business speakers. Holli has more than 25 years of experience managing and growing the businesses of our industry's best. Holli and her team have partnered with countless corporations, associations, bureaus, and speakers across the nation to earn a reputation for superior service, integrity, and excellence through collaboration. In April 2010, Holli was honored with the IASB John Palmer Award for exemplary service to the bureau industry. She can be reached at holli@speakersoffice.com or www.speakersoffice.com.

HOW TO SPICE UP YOUR WRITING

Dianna Booher, MA, CSP, CPAE

What does your writing say about your brand? For all the words speakers deliver from the platform, they write far more frequently—and often less fluently. They write client proposals, query letters and e-mail to editors and agents, articles, book proposals, books, contracts, marketing plans, business plans, blogs, e-mail, tweets, audio scripts, video scripts, website copy, brochure copy, packaging copy, workbooks, and handouts. Occasionally, they may even write a speech or a check.

Even with all that practice, there are ways to improve writing skill, speed—and confidence.

PLAN BIG PROJECTS IN SMALL STEPS.

Journalists or novelists do not wait until an editor's deadline looms before hitting the keyboard. Instead, they lay out the project by steps. For any given project, the steps might look like this: Do secondary research. Survey. Analyze survey results. Brainstorm article angle. Interview. Do primary research on location. Request photos and artwork. Draft. Edit. Ask colleagues to review. Complete final edit.

A speaker's project should be no different—waiting until a book deadline creeps onto the month-at-a-glance calendar courts disaster and leaves no time for leisurely reviews and editing. Write-from-the-gut-and-go is no way to showcase one's best thinking for the next decade.

ORGANIZE CONTENT WITH IDEA WHEELS.

Try the idea wheel as an outlining tool for speed and efficiency. Idea wheels can facilitate brainstorming and outlining an entire 50,000-word business book in a couple of hours; planning and drafting website content, or structuring a client proposal, can be accomplished even more swiftly.

British psychologist Tony Buzan originated the idea of mind-mapping®. His concept-mapping technique works well for categorizing the unstructured

Figure 17-1.

As a brainstorming tool, idea wheels allow you to capture fleeting ideas as they occur. For a writing tool, reorder them sequentially as a second step BEFORE you draft.

free flow of ideas and information. In the early 1980s, I built on Buzan's idea when I wrote about idea wheels—for the purpose of the initial free flow of ideas that must eventually end up in a linear document. Although all such diagrams (branching, clustering, fish bones) look similar, there are three major distinctions with idea wheels: structure, subordination, and sequence. The idea wheel helps to distinguish major points from minor points and to sequence the spokes on the wheel in a specific order.

In short, this technique captures random thoughts quickly, and then reorders them easily in a first draft. It starts with a key concept written inside a circle (or wheel hub). Breaking down that broad concept results in spokes from the hub, and sub-points can be drawn as spokes from the spokes. Repetitive points can be rearranged immediately into the appropriate spoke.

If a chart starts to run off the page, the spoke can be turned into another wheel hub and the process can be repeated. After every idea has been captured on the page, it's time to assign letters and numbers (like outlining in high-school English class, IA, IB, IIA, IIB and so on). This puts a sequential order on the brainstorming, making it usable for the document draft.

Don't worry about starting off "right"—the idea-wheel technique is designed to generate a good volume of ideas quickly. If absolutely nothing comes to mind, start off with "who," "what," "why," "where," "how," and "how much" on the wheel spokes. Then go from there. If every detail seems to spin off the "why" spoke, then start over with another idea wheel, using "why" as the hub. (Figure 17-1 arranges brainstormed ideas into a more logical and usable format.)

Use Idea Wheels for Organizing Longer Documents.

Remember: Idea wheels differ from mind maps in three important ways:

- *Sequence*: Decide the logical order before drafting.
- *Structure*: Make all structures look like wheels with spokes.
- *Subordination*: Use similar structure to quickly distinguish major ideas from supporting ideas.

Those differences can save enormous amounts of time in writing "lean" on the first draft of any proposal, speech, article, or book.

SET THE PACE ACCORDING TO THE PURPOSE.

Speakers consider their audiences when formulating a core message—and may even adjust their delivery style and dress to fit the audience's mood, attitude, and venue.

When it comes to writing, however, some people have a "one-size-fits-all" approach. That is, their books sound like their articles, which sound like their blogs, which sound like their marketing materials, which sound like their proposals, which sound like their client e-mail.

Documents need a life of their own. Consider these four essentials to select the appropriate style and pace for any particular document: 1) the message, 2) the purpose, 3) the reader, and 4) the relationship to the reader.

As an example, consider two different kinds of nonfiction: a business book aimed at executives and a general inspirational book. The typical business book will have:

- concise chapter summaries
- frequent informative headings to allow for skimming
- several key points per chapter
- a few case studies or illustrations per chapter
- statistics, studies, data

The typical inspirational book aimed at a general audience will have:

- few, if any, chapter summaries
- no headings within the chapters—or perhaps uninformative, teaser headings
- only one or two key points per chapter
- many illustrations and examples for each key point
- personal experiences rather than case studies, statistics, or other data to support key points

In the above lists, notice the compression of information—or lack thereof. That's the essence of pacing. How fast are you feeding the reader information? How easily accessible is the information? How many times do you "make the point" before the reader has to "get the point" before you "move beyond the point"? That's the point about pace.

Neither pace for information flow is superior; they simply differ as to what's appropriate for the purpose.

SUMMARIZE WELL.

Make your bottom line your opening line. That's particularly true when writing proposals to senior executives. In reviewing documents from our proposal writing workshops for corporate clients, we've discovered a common challenge: Some writers confuse a purpose statement with a message statement.

> **Purpose Statement:** "Smith Consulting is pleased to provide this proposal to lead your organization to develop its own system for innovation. Your managers will learn to overcome challenges they face and understand the actions they need to take to remain competitive."

> **Message Statement:** "Smith Consulting is pleased to provide this proposal for a series of six interactive programs to lead your managers to develop their personal system for calculating risk, making sound decisions, and addressing challenges with innovative solutions. They will explore the challenges of retaining top talent, cost-cutting, and marketing to a fragmented customer base. Your audience will walk away with innovative actions to implement in the next 30 days in all three areas."

MATCH ELABORATION TO EMPHASIS.
Space equals importance.

In our technical writing workshops, this principle typically catches writers off guard—particularly engineers and auditors. Like the rest of us, they tend to write the most about what they know best and feel most passionate about—and that may not be of most interest to the decision maker buying a widget or the manager charged with changing a process after an unfavorable audit.

Take a closer look at your own proposals and website copy. Have you spent the most words and space on the most important ideas? Would your readers agree?

If you offer three key benefits to the client, and you spend 350 words on benefit A and 300 words on benefit B, and 20 words on benefit C, then you're telling the client that benefit C is far less important than the first two. Is that true? If not, adjust your copy.

Use informative headings to tell your story.

Would a newspaper ever use headlines like these—"The President," "Congress," "Unemployment," or "Murder"? Of course not. Neither do headings such as "Terms" or "Scheduling" in proposals inform buyers. Prefer specific, informative headings rather than vague, general ones. Examples: "Schedule for Transferring Learning to Action" or "Unique Approach to Coaching Your Executives."

The most important headings most of us create daily? E-mail subject lines. Make them significant yet succinct.

Write lean; trim the fat.

Be ruthless about ridding writing of riff-raff that dilutes key points. Cut every unnecessary word. Many words add absolutely nothing but length. (Notice that *absolutely* in the previous sentence adds emphasis; therefore, it remains.)

Trimming clichés, redundancies, and weak-verb padding makes writing emphatic and crisp. But finding the fat in your own work can be exacting. Phrases that "roll off your tongue" "with little or no effort" (as the last two phrases just rolled off mine) are a clue that you're using clichés.

Sentences that incorporate redundant words and ideas seem even more difficult to recognize than clichés. For instance, *continue on. To continue* means *to go on*; when you add the *on*, you're stuttering. "If you can't spell *accommodations*, run the spellchecker to verify it." The entire last idea is redundant: "If you can't spell *accommodations*, run the spellchecker."

Little-word padding also clutters messages. Notice how deleting the italicized phrases creates better sentences:

> The number of ideas generated from the program can be attributed to *various factors such as* market size, labor problems, and management philosophy.

> Better: The number of ideas generated from the program can be attributed to market size, labor problems, and management philosophy.

The attached questionnaire is for *your use in* providing the necessary information for the upcoming keynote.

Better: The attached questionnaire is for providing the necessary information for the upcoming keynote.

The client *is a man who* dislikes ultimatums and irresponsibility.

Better: The client dislikes ultimatums and irresponsibility.

In spite of the fact that he offered full fee, we have *decided to* decline the invitation to appear before that audience.

Better: Despite his full-fee offer, we have declined his invitation to appear before that audience.

William Strunk, in *The Elements of Style*, said it best: "A sentence should contain no unnecessary words, a paragraph no unnecessary sentences, for the same reason that a drawing should have no unnecessary lines and a machine no unnecessary parts."

Stir in the spice.

What adds punch to keynotes also breathes life into writing—even when it's how-tos and hard business data: Alliteration. Rhythm. Pithy quotations. Provocative questions. Illustrations and examples. Humor. Personal experiences. Anecdotes. Mnemonic devices. Analogies and metaphors. In fact, the more technical the topic, the more seasoning is required to entice the reader to finish.

Even then, attention and comprehension may be a struggle—as I learned early in my career. I had just finished a two-day event for a utility company in which I'd presented my proprietary MADE Format® for writing business documents, with each letter of the acronym representing a section of the standard document. As part of the case study, I asked attendees to review a one-page recap of that format from my book. A few minutes later as we ended the session, the client asked participants to mention the most useful takeaways from the session.

One manager spoke up in all sincerity, "This was the best program I've ever attended in all my 30 years on the job. I'm going to use this format every day in everything I write. This M. A.... this M. D. A." Flustered, she paused a moment, glancing around the room to locate the flipchart where I'd written the MADE acronym, then continued, "That format — the M. E.... the A. M. E. D. No, that's not it. Well, you know, whatever it is. I'll never forget it."

For all the effort and despite the spice, moments like this keep writers and speakers humble.

Get rid of the grammar gremlins.

George Carlin made a career of oddities in the English language. He delivered entire routines around queries such as, "Why do we park on driveways and drive on parkways?" People laughed and paid him. Write oddities (outright mistakes that suggest that you don't understand the language) and people will laugh—but they won't want to pay you!

Here's a list of common mistakes that appear in books, articles, e-mail, proposals, tweets, brochures, and website copy:

Hi Mike (A comma must set off a name when you address a person directly: *Hi, Mike*)

Other clients who have contracted with us for customized programs, include Pepsico and Raytheon. (Punctuation error— comma erroneously inserted between the subject and verb of the sentence)

The room setup will effect the group dynamics for such programs..." (Misused word: should be *affect*)

There's many reasons for choosing a speaker with experience in the industry. (wrong verb: should be *There are*)

I can give you an explanation of my fee rather quick, and then we can talk in more detail later in the week. (*quick* should be *quickly*)

He objected to the delay in surveying the client, and the fact he failed to notify us that he would be attending the evening event. (parallelism error)

The pricing in the contract contains a cancellation clause that is good for 90 days for all participating speakers and entertainers, which has not been approved by the speaker bureau. (What has not been approved? The clause? The contract? The pricing?)

People do judge a book by its cover. Decision makers do judge a speaker by his or her proposals, e-mail, blogs, website copy, or proposals. Audiences do judge a training course by its workbook or handout. Improper grammar matters as much as appropriate dress or an engaging delivery on the platform.

Writing is part of your brand. Don't make it bland.

Dianna Booher, MA, CSP, CPAE, helps organizations increase productivity and improve effectiveness through better communication: oral, written, interpersonal, and cross-functional. She's the author of 44 books (Random House, Simon & Schuster, McGraw-Hill), published in 23 countries, in 16 languages. Several have been selections by major book clubs: Newbridge, Macmillan Executive, Book-of-the-Month/Fortune, Writers Digest. Her latest titles include *The Voice of Authority: 10 Communication Strategies Every Leader Needs to Know* and *Booher's Rules of Business Grammar: 101 Fast and Easy Ways to Correct the Most Common Errors.* For more information, visit www.booher.com or contact her at dianna.booher@booher.com.

LAND THAT BOOK CONTRACT!

Rich Gallagher

Most public speakers have at least a book or two in them. Today, there are more opportunities than ever to have a book out there, with the growth of new publishing channels and print-on-demand technology. And for many people, the top of the mountain is to land a contract with a major publisher—and the chance to see their message on the shelves of bookstores around the country.

Every journey begins with a first step, and in fact, the following few pages provide four of them toward landing a contract with a mainstream publisher. It's the ideal path for speakers who want to put the resources of an entire publishing industry behind them and their careers.

STEP 1. STUDYING THE GENRE

Everyone has read books that changed their lives. Before a speaker even thinks of putting finger to keyboard, it's time to get those books out, and start looking at them with a new pair of eyes.

Here's why: A book pitch to an agent or publisher has less than a minute or two to make a good impression. And one of the first things they're looking for is that "published author" aura. Breaking down successful books' style and structure can help reverse engineer the components that great published authors put into the mix.

Most books from major publishers fall into certain genres that have their own format and rhythm. The big genres, of course, are things like non-fiction business or life-improvement books. Beneath that, there are sub-genres that describe whole classes of books: for example, publishers may refer to a title as a "seven steps" book (even if it actually has four or sixteen steps), a business fable, or a thought leadership book.

The difference between being a self-published and published author often revolves around studying the genre. Many self-published authors simply turn on the word processor, start writing whatever comes to mind, and then stop 30,000 or 50,000 words later. By comparison, most published books are thoughtfully composed performances that reflect the genre they are published in.

Chapter structure, paragraph lengths, and opening hooks of other successful books are all part of essential research. An aspiring author who wants to write the next *Who Moved My Cheese?* needs to create something no longer than 25,000 words, broken up into easily digestible sections and plot points, that teaches a lesson usually laid out in three or four parts. In contrast, someone following in the footsteps of a weighty tome such as *The Wisdom of Crowds* will need to clock in at over 80,000 words and have two or three detailed case studies per chapter. And those seeking to break the mold of established book genres—far and away the hardest way to get published—need to make sure they're choosing this path on purpose and not by accident.

Next comes the question of style. In the communications skills field, some books just lay it out straight: "This chapter will tell you how to communicate in X situation." Others weave a story line around the same point: "Megan was in tears after John came home and didn't ask about her day." Different genres have different styles. That doesn't mean exactly mimicking the specifics of a genre, but it's a good idea to understand the landscape first.

Then there's gut instinct. How do your favorite books affect you? Are they informative? Engaging? Easy to read? If they are telling a story, do they bring out emotions? Finally, get on Amazon and see how well other books sell. The right structure and a good competitive analysis are the two most valuable elements in a successful book proposal.

STEP 2. THE RULE OF ONES

Some people may not realize that marketing a nonfiction book to publishers doesn't actually mean writing the book first. The first item that needs to be written is a book proposal, which is then used to secure a contract to write the book. The success or failure of a book proposal is ultimately tied to three elements: one line, one page, and one chapter.

The one line is your title. Why did you purchase your last book? In all likelihood, because its title attracted you. When Tim Ferris decided to title his book *The 4-Hour Workweek*, he had already done most of the work of creating a best seller. The title is the brand—the more it grabs people, and the closer it ties in with a speaker's platform, the stronger the chances of placing it with a publisher. This one line has more to do with success than the tens of thousands of words that will follow.

With titles, simplicity is key. Think of top sellers that have stood the test of time: *The Tipping Point. Crucial Conversations. Think and Grow Rich. How to Win Friends and Influence People.* In almost every case, the content of the book—and its benefit to the reader—is immediately clear from the title. There are exceptions, of course, but the author who wants to call her masterpiece *The Dream of the Blue Elephant* will have some explaining to do. And publishers and agents are generally not good at offering the opportunity to explain.

The one page is the query. This generally takes the form of a short e-mail—a first contact with an agent or publisher. Write a great one, and the chances of getting to write the book go up substantially. Write a stale or trite one, and even Kurt Vonnegut wouldn't get a callback. Strong queries will invariably lead to book editors and agents asking to see additional work—in other words, out of the slush pile and into the inner sanctum.

This can be accomplished with a short, one-page query with three bullet-item paragraphs in the body of it:

- What my book is about, including its title and target market.
- Why my book is important: a quick, one-paragraph competitive and market analysis
- Why I'm the right person to write it: a summary of my writing and business credentials that are relevant to this book project.

That's it. No gimmicks, nothing cute, and no beating around the bush—just a short, readable summary of benefits that can be scanned in 30 seconds or less. Master these three paragraphs, and it dramatically boosts the opportunity to write lots more pages. This is an example from a successful query:

> **About the Book**: *Great Customer Connections* is designed to do for customer transactions what *The New York Times* best seller *Crucial Conversations* did for conflict management—present a literate, well-researched look at the behavioral psychology that drives customer interactions, while giving readers specific

communication tools that dramatically change the success of these interactions.

Target Audience: This book is targeted at the high end of front-line service professionals and the people who manage them. Its methodology has created dramatic real-life results, including near-perfect customer satisfaction levels, near-zero turnover, and high sales growth. Its approach is now being incorporated as part of a campus-wide customer service initiative at Cornell University, and it has been taught to thousands of people nationwide.

About the Author: I am a full-time writer and corporate trainer with an award-winning 20-plus-year career in the customer contact industry. My five nationally published books include (. . .). I am a consummate professional who cooperates with editors, promotes creatively and aggressively, and never, ever misses a deadline!

Finally, the one chapter is a sample of the work. The title and query are arguably more important than the chapter content, but it is here that authors show who they are and what they know. This chapter can be one of the "meat" chapters from the middle of the book; if possible, consider combining it with an introductory section that frames the book's value proposition.

The title, pitch, and chapter samples then become part of a larger book proposal, which includes other content such as the table of contents, chapter summaries, a marketing plan for the book, biography, and platform. One particularly important section of this proposal is the competitive analysis mentioned earlier, which frames where the book stands against other successful books. Look at examples of good proposals from resources (some examples are listed in the next section), keep workshopping until it is truly incredible, and have it ready to go on a moment's notice when people respond positively to a query.

STEP 3. PITCHING YOUR PRODUCT

Now comes the fun part: marketing the work to agents or publishers.

The first decision is whether to use a literary agent or not, depending on the envisioned market. Some publishers, such as many business trade publishers, are willing to hear directly from authors. Others, such as the large New York imprints, will only accept agented submissions.

In most cases, it's worth trying to find an agent first. Good ones are worth every penny of their commission and more. First and foremost, they provide an entree to all of the major publishers. Second, their expertise in negotiating book contracts is critical for speakers. For example, speakers have special needs, such as audio rights and ancillary training products, that need to be built into the contract. Finally, a good agent relationship can become an important part of a speaker's long-term platform.

Let's boil the marketing process down into numbers. Resources such as *Writer's Market* show that many agents accept less than 5 percent of the projects pitched to them. Don't get depressed by these figures. Here's why: Most queries and book proposals are *terrible*. Many people simply want to get published, versus learning the mechanics of doing it well. After subtracting all those truly awful pitches, that 4 percent suddenly looks more like a comfortable double-digit number—and multiplied across the number of agents out there, an aspiring author's chances are looking much better.

The query for *Great Customer Connections*, excerpted above, was originally sent via e-mail to approximately 30 agents in early 2004. (I was "between agents" at the time, following the passing of my previous agent.) Of these 30 agents:

- Fifteen sent a rejection by e-mail, most within 48 hours.
- Eight never responded.
- Seven asked to see a copy of my proposal
- Two of these agents eventually offered to represent it.

The agent I selected then sent my proposal to an initial group of 12 major business publishers, 10 of whom rejected it, and two of whom were interested in it. We chose AMACOM because of its track record with customer service books and their overseas distribution channels. I signed a contract in November 2004 and was given until mid-May 2005 to finish the book (which I did, at 5:00 a.m., two days before the deadline).

As for the contacts themselves, two of my favorite resources are *Writer's Market* and *Jeff Herman's Guide to Book Publishers, Editors, and Literary Agents*. Both are chock-full of up-to-date contact information as well as practical advice on successful proposals. The former can be purchased with access to an online database of contacts, while the latter has some of the best content I've seen on successful publishing. Speakers who are serious about writing should treat themselves to both of these resources.

One last point about marketing. Would anyone hire an assistant whose e-mail began with "Dear speaker"? Never, ever send a query or proposal to a generic title such as "Editor"—even if that's what the publisher's website instructs. Get on the phone and get real names of editors or agents. Better yet, be prepared to make a brief elevator pitch if they happen to answer. Then get those queries out.

STEP 4. THE CONSUMMATE PROFESSIONAL

Those who might think that the most important factor in success as a writer is writing are wrong. Writers are in the business of communicating with other people, and when it comes to succeeding in this business for the long haul, how others see you as a person ranks way over your prose.

There are two things that separate professional writers from non-pros. The first and most obvious one is the mechanics: meeting deadlines, getting the word count right, doing what's promised, and all the other things that are fundamental to any business relationship. Good writers have to be in the business of pleasing their clients, just like any other profession.

The second and more subtle point is how a writer works with others. The popular misconception of writing a book is toiling in silence on it for months or years, heaving it over a very high wall, and then seeing it magically appear on a bookshelf. In reality, there are networks of people at every step of the publishing process, including agents, editors, copyeditors, cover artists, and publicists—and they are all, well, human. And what they think about an author will affect his or her writing career every bit as much as how well the chapters read.

Writing, like any business, has its frustrations. Editors will change favorite passages. Publishers will design a loud, ugly cover. Agents may take months or years trying to get a book placed with a publisher. Publicists may only be able to get airtime in Sheboygan instead of on Oprah. Handling these frustrations and day-to-day interactions with these people has a much greater influence on the future than one might realize. Be polite, professional, and cooperative, and the rewards will come back many times over in good working relationships and more publishing opportunities.

BONUS STEP: A LOOK IN THE MIRROR

There really is a process to landing a publishing contract. At the same time, the most important part of getting published occurs with a glance in the mirror each morning. Is that person saying, "I love to write" . . . or "I'd like to get published, but this sounds like a lot of work"? Those who truly love to write should follow that passion. That, in itself, will guide anxious authors through the waiting, the rejections, the drafts, and the deadlines, and, in all likelihood, reward them with the pleasure of seeing their own books on the shelf.

Rich Gallagher heads Point of Contact Group (www.pointofcontactgroup.com), a training and development firm that has taught more than 10,000 people what to say in their most difficult workplace situations. A former customer service executive with a track record of dramatically "turning around" the performance of customer contact operations, his eight books include the national #1 customer service best seller, *What to Say to a Porcupine*, and his latest book, *How to Tell Anyone Anything*. He is also a ghostwriter and writing coach, and can be reached at www.YourOnlineWritingCoach. com.

USE VERBAL PING-PONG TO GET A RISE FROM YOUR ELEVATOR SPEECH

Brian Walter, CSP

Every week, a professional speaker is going to be asked the single most opportunity-laden, open-ended inquiry anyone can hear: "What do you do?"

The embarrassing truth is that deep down, most speakers fear the question—because most of the time, they've stumble-bumbled through it or subtly tried to avoid it, because what they've got prepared isn't working.

A question that should be professionally stimulating (and a wellspring of future gigs) turns into an ongoing source of stress. That's because the stakes are very clear when this simple, conversational question is asked.

What comes out of a speaker's mouth next determines the difference between an interesting expert worthy of follow-up or referral ("Hey, give me your card") or as one step above a rabid, multilevel salesperson ("Oh, look at the time, gotta go!").

So if everyone knows this, what's the deal? The problem is that most speakers create their elevator speeches on a flawed premise. The solution is to take a conceptual detour from nearly all the elevator speech systems out there. Here's the big shift . . .

An elevator *speech* is not an elevator *pitch*.

When someone asks, "What do you do?" they're not actually saying "Hey, speaker-person-I-just-met, would you sell me really hard right now?" But if that's how the question is answered, the inquiring party is going to hit the emergency stop button and toss the hard-seller right off their own elevator.

Let's get the context right. This isn't about official sales calls. An elevator speech is designed for people or prospects in informal situations. So the big shift requires redefining the goal:

> An elevator speech is a progressively revealed conversational answer to the question *What do you do?*, delivered in such a way that people want you to *keep* talking.

The immediate goal isn't a sale; it's creating interest. Does the person want to know more? Excellent things can happen when that's the case. Here's the new elevator speech definition broken out by conceptual piece.

" . . . A PROGRESSIVELY REVEALED . . ."

Progressively revealed means there's no need to cover the entire value proposition in one giant rushed elevator speech diatribe. How many seconds should it take? Less than most people realize.

The consensus of most marketing and communication books is that an elevator speech should be between 15 and 60 seconds. The average is 30 seconds. That sounds right . . . but only on paper. The problem occurs when all of that comes out of your mouth—no matter what the words are. Try it. Pull out a stopwatch or even just look at the second hand on your watch or a clock. Ask yourself "So what do you do?" in a perky enthusiastic way. And then time yourself, just saying "blah-blah-blah-blah-blah." This simulates your answer to the question time-wise, without distracting you about the actual content itself.

It doesn't take long to get boring. The stark reality is 30 seconds or even 15 seconds is too much. It takes about three. Naturally, an entire elevator speech can't be delivered in three seconds . . . assuming the *entire* thing is being conveyed at one time. But that's not how it works.

Delivering a memorable elevator speech is about aggressively avoiding a monologue. An elevator speech needs to be expressed as a dialogue—like a game of verbal Ping-Pong.

The other person starts by serving the ball with "What do you do?"

Most of the time, the return volley goes like this: "Gee, thanks for asking. I'm going to talk for a while now. You might want to sit down."

To which the victim returns: "Noooooo!"

Game over.

No one wants to play that way. The savvy speaker hits it back to someone with a short answer—rather than grabbing and holding on to the ball. Having a bit of back and forth creates a comfortable, natural way to progressively reveal expertise. Thus, the person who asked the question doesn't feel like they are the victim of a verbal onslaught. Instead, it's game on.

"... CONVERSATIONAL ANSWER ..."

Conversational answer simply means speaking like normal people, not an article in *The Wall Street Journal*. How unfortunately familiar does this sound?

"What do I do? Well, I'm a leadership expert with MegaImpact Inc., where I deliver maximum value through value-added dynamic processes and people-oriented systems, as well as fully integrated productivity programs which achieve measurable world-class ROI results that can be escalated to meet the increasing needs of an increasingly complex business environment that demands precision, professionalism and something else that starts with the letter P."

In an informal situation, that's a simply freakish way to answer. The Straight Face Test will prove it.

Stand in front of a mirror and ask yourself, "What do you do?" Then see if you can keep a straight face while spouting your usual spiel. If you find yourself smirking, twitching, stuttering, laughing out loud, rolling your eyes, or thinking *"This is such B.S."*... that's a sign. It's time to remove the business buzzwords, keep the six normal words, and start over.

"... THAT YOU DELIVER IN SUCH A WAY THAT PEOPLE WANT YOU TO KEEP TALKING ..."

This part of the elevator speech definition is the most critical. Everyone's familiar with the concept of "permission marketing," which means that you legally can't send people business e-mail without their permission. They must electronically opt in to receiving information. An elevator speech is "permission talking"—the other person needs to opt in to what's being said.

Opted-in listeners cock their heads or raise an eyebrow. Or grunt out a "Huh, what? Hmm." Or what I call the Scooby-Doo response: "Baaaargh?" That kind of nonverbal reaction means they've hit the Ping-Pong ball back. It's permission to keep talking.

Deep down, people really do want to respond. And it's easy when someone has a killer response such as:

"I build the guidance systems in Space Shuttles."

"I train Navy Seals."

"I actually am a rocket scientist."

A professional speaker's reply may not seem that cool, but speaking topics can still be sexy! Remember, someone asked "What do you do?" because they had an initial interest. So don't stop being interesting during the ensuing conversation. And you achieve that by following the simple Verbal Ping Pong Elevator Speech formula: WOW, HOW, NOW.

The WOW is the first one-sentence answer to "What do you do?" It's designed to elicit the Scooby-Doo response. Then comes HOW—a sentence or two job description (speaker, consultant, coach, trainer) along with one benefit or at least the hint of a benefit. After that comes the NOW, which is the start of the three of the most powerful words in the English language: *"Now, for example."* Because that's the start of a story, much better than "Once upon a time." Everyone likes a good story. Especially if it's short.

For speakers, the elevator speech opportunity connects the listener to the speaker's Big Concept. Stepping outside the speaker world illustrates this clearly, using the example of a sales rep for a fictitious automatic defibrillator company called HeartMax Technologies.

> **The Question:** "So, what do you do?"
> **WOW Response:** "I'm in the human jumper-cable business."

Bam! Short and intriguing. That's a spectacular WOW line, a guaranteed hook. Why? Because *human jumper cable business* sounds reeeeally interesting.

It would be pretty much impossible for someone to actually stop listening. They have to know more, signaled with the Scooby-Doo response or a follow-up query. Time to jump to the HOW line.

> **HOW Response:** "I work for HeartMax Technology . . . it's my

job to get our automatic defibrillator units, like those paddle things on ER (mime zapping), into companies and schools."

Now they've got a visual image, and are thinking, "Oh, so *that's* what he meant by human jumper cables," followed by a comment or more head nodding. That's permission to say another line . . . with a benefit.

> **Benefit Reinforcement:** "So normal *nonmedical* people, like you and me, can actually save the lives of our co-workers and kids."

At this point, most people will go "Oh, that's interesting" or put on their *New York Face*, which means . . . Okay, you're done. But sometimes they'll be hooked and want more of the details. With those people, the next step is a compelling real-world story that starts with the new three most powerful words in your business vocabulary, "Now, for example . . ."

Once the story begins, the elevator speech is over. This is what behavioral scientists call . . . a conversation. Maybe that will lead to a "give me your card" situation, or even a request to set up a meeting, but maybe it won't. At the very least, an indelible impression has been made.

"NOW, FOR EXAMPLE," PART II

An elevator speech isn't a selling conversation, it's a preselling conversation. WOW, HOW, NOW might lead to something, but it starts with just talking. And simply because someone expresses interest in an elevator speech doesn't mean they're interested in being sold to . . . yet. That's where "Now, for example" comes into play.

There are five different selling story formats to consider, depending on the goal: displaying industry knowledge, establishing credibility, tying in to an odd speaking topic, demonstrating work style, or creating emotional connection. The formats to achieve this are: Train Wreck, Name Dropper, Surfer Dude, Movie Trailer, and Star Maker.

Train Wreck

The Train Wreck story is all about the problem, not the solution. The person gets to vicariously enjoy the pain of someone else who could have used help, but didn't. It's a way of proving an understanding of a potential client's industry or workplace reality by articulating it rather than simply saying, "I get it."

Name Dropper

The second story format is the "Name Dropper" technique: a casual mention of an extremely high-profile company that's a past client. The goal is to subtly communicate"if-we're-good-enough-for-them-we're-more-than-good-enough-for-you." Instant credibility.

Surfer Dude

This format is all about the simile . . . describing what a speaker's style or topic is *like* through a familiar cultural reference. ("I'm like a combination of Dr. Phil and Robin Williams on referral selling.") Make sure it's fast, easy to grasp, and not too obscure.

Movie Trailer

Imagine a deep-throated voiceover artist saying, "In a world full of boring speakers who drone on and on . . . comes a really fast-paced example of just the good stuff of what I have done for people like you!" The Movie Trailer describes scene snippets of expertise in action, brief word-picture glimpses of the speaking equivalent of car chases, explosions, funny lines, and love scenes—capturing their attention so they want to see the whole thing!

Star Maker

This is the most sophisticated of the formats. It's a narrated scene, just like the Movie Trailer, but starring the person you're talking to—placed right into the story, called by name, making choices and decisions, receiving benefits, and ending up as the hero.

ENJOY THE GAME.

Clearly, a lot of time and thought goes into a short, effective elevator speech strategy. Write it out, say it, edit it, practice it, and enjoy knowing that it's going to work when it's time to play Verbal Ping-Pong. A bit of strategy and just a few short, memorized lines will prepare any speaker to answer "What do you do?" in a fashion that eliminates fear—and keeps the conversation action going.

Brian Walter, CSP, is a communication consultant and corporate humorist. He runs Extreme Meetings®, which provides customized infotainment to make meetings memorable. For more information, visit www.extrememeetings.com or contact him at brian@extrememeetings.com.

YOUR NAME IN LIGHTS! HOW TO CAPITALIZE ON THE POWER OF PUBLICITY

Pam Lontos, MA, CSP

Publicity can be as simple as having a letter published on the op-ed page of the local newspaper, as splashy as a front-page article with your name in the headline, or as savvy as appearing at the top of search engine results. While many people understand the power of publicity, they often don't know how to use it to their advantage. Building publicity is important to your speaking career because it will allow you to command higher fees, sell more books and other products, and gain more bookings.

But remember, smart publicity is not a one-time effort that results in fifteen minutes of fame. For publicity to pay off, you must have a long-term strategy that builds your credibility as an expert, makes you known to your target audience, and creates lasting examples of your message.

Realize that one interview or TV appearance won't make you a best seller or in-demand speaker. People need to see your name six or seven times before they actually remember it. By creating your hook, positioning yourself as an expert to the media, gaining print media placements, and engaging in a professional online and social media campaign, you can use the power of publicity to elevate your speaking career to the next level.

The following information and activities will help you get started on your publicity and on your way to seeing your name everywhere.

WHAT'S YOUR HOOK?

The reason audiences and the media are compelled to listen to a speaker, read his or her book, or learn more about the speaker is because they are intrigued by his or her "hook." Your hook is what defines you as unique; it's what makes the press want to talk to you, meeting managers want to book you, and clients want to hire you. Maybe you are going against the grain of societal thought. Maybe you can offer your audience advice that will change their lives. By developing a good hook and using it in your press releases, media kit, and website, you will gain greater interest from those who can hire you.

A good hook is catchy, timely, and sustainable. While that may seem contradictory on the surface, it isn't. Your expertise and brand are what make you sustainable; your ability to relate to the audience is what must be timely; and your ability to prove yourself above others is why you must be catchy.

When push comes to shove, reporters and producers don't care about

Activity: Creating a Hook

1. What is your base? (e.g., Hippy Housewife, Best Salesman Ever, GeekChic)_____

_____

2. What makes you different? (e.g., you have a successful product, you scaled Mount Everest while whistling Yankee Doodle Dandy)

_____

3. Who is your audience? (men, women, sports enthusiasts, knitters)

_____

4. What current news items can you comment on?_____

_____

5. What practical advice can you give?_____

_____

your product or service—they are interested only in how you can make their publication or show more appealing to their audience. Therefore, your hook should address the needs of a particular media outlet's readers or viewers. And each outlet you pitch should get its own unique hook congruent with its unique audience. Adaptation is the foundation for creating your hook.

MAKE YOURSELF THE EXPERT

Writing articles based on your expertise for industry publications, op-eds in the newspaper, and other print media sources provides you the ability to establish yourself as an expert and to market your speaking in the author's bio. Print media have a long-lasting effect on your publicity because they stay around. Print media also carry credibility for their authors because editors choose them for publication.

Like any marketing effort, your focus with publicity should be on reaching the decision makers. When you are published in industry, trade, association, and business newspapers, you are reaching those people who have the authority in their companies to make the expenditures to hire you to speak. CEOs and other decision makers will read industry-specific magazines cover to cover, which allow them to see your name and your bio.

Writing articles that magazines want to publish is an art. Remember that as in any other form of media, print editors want articles that will allow them to meet their circulation and ad sales goals. You must show them specifically why your article will help and engage their readership. Your articles should never self-promote, should not be written in the first person, and should contain good content, not fluff.

The formula for an article that magazines want to publish is simple. Create a provocative title that relates to your content. Begin with a great opening sentence and follow with a story or illustrative scenario. (Don't use real names, though, if the story is based on an actual client; that's a no-no.) Use the second paragraph to relate the dilemma to the readers. The next short paragraphs should consist of three to eight tips, strategies, or steps the reader can take to solve the problem. Finally, summarize your advice and solutions in one paragraph with a call to action at the end. Keep the word count around 800 to 1,000 words or about 2.5 pages.

Perhaps the most often overlooked, but immensely important, part of publishing print articles is creating your resource box, where you put your contact information. These two to three sentences should include multiple ways to contact you such as website, phone number, and e-mail address.

Make sure to mention that you are available for speaking engagements, not just your company, service, or well-known clients. Space allowing, you may also mention any books or products you have.

Getting interviewed in newsstand publications also helps raise your publicity. Use your expertise to contact reporters and pitch yourself as newsworthy and

Activity: Creating Your Article Outline

1. Nail your provocative title:_____

_____

2. Create your opening sentence and story: _____

_____

3. Identify the benefits to the reader: _____

_____

4. List your tips or advice: (1)_____

(2)_____

(3)_____

(4)_____

5. Summarize your content and call readers to action to remedy the problem:_____

_____

_____

6. Create your resource box: _____

_____

_____

Activity: Preparing Your Media Pitch

List three general topics you can be an expert on for interviews:

_____

_____

_____

List the top five newsstand media you will pitch your story to (e.g.,
Newsweek, MarieClaire, Redbook, The Wall Street Journal):

_____

_____

_____

List three timely story lines that you can be interviewed on. Then list
the three main points that you will have ready during the interview.

(1)_____

   a._____

   b._____

   c._____

(2)_____

   a._____

   b._____

   c._____

(3)_____

   a._____

   b._____

   c._____

quotable. Even if the reporter's topic isn't directly related to your main speaking topic, getting your name out there, especially in recognized publications like *The Wall Street Journal*, *Cosmopolitan*, or *USA Today*, will still help raise your publicity and help you form relationships with the media who will then call you when a story breaks directly in your line of expertise.

When planning your publicity approach for getting interviewed, don't fall into the trap of thinking you can't get into large publications. In reality, writers scramble daily to find people to interview who have knowledge on the latest issues and trends. Also, remember that small publications do matter. Even if the reporter writes for a small-town newspaper, his or her story can be picked up through press news services and be more widely distributed. Never say no to an opportunity for press coverage; you never know where it might take you.

Remember to pitch a story or offer advice for a reporter's audience rather than focus on yourself. Always highlight the benefits for the audience. Pitching yourself won't get you anywhere. On the same note, always answer the reporter's questions directly, and never refer them to your book or products to find the answer. Your job during an interview is to help the reporter help his or her audience, not to self-promote. Being quoted as an expert will do the promotion for you and your speaking career.

ONLINE AND SOCIAL MEDIA FOR SPEAKERS

Social media and online publicity are two of the ways you can increase your publicity and reach to your prospective audience. To ensure that social media and being online work for you in a positive way, the following guidelines will help.

Online publicity begins with your website. Every speaker needs a website; it's not optional anymore. You can either have a website that is solely for the purposes of your speaking career or, if you also have a business that ties into your speaking topic, a page promoting your speaking on your company's website. Whichever option you choose, this site will be the spot your social media efforts and resource box link to.

An important element to include on your website is a cleanly written biography that includes your relevant education and work experience. With their permission, include a list of current and past clients, along with their industry type to show your core strengths. Clients are also a great source of testimonials for your service that, with permission, should also be displayed. Include a list of topics and presentation titles you offer on a routine basis and indicate whether you can create custom presentations. Also, make sure to have a page that highlights and links to all of that great publicity you have from getting interviewed and publishing articles.

Organize and present multimedia on your website to best show your ability to deliver on what you promise. Using video clips or audio recordings help show meeting planners that you can be dynamic, informative, and engaging—all of the things they are looking for. Using multimedia wisely (i.e., not over-cluttering your pages and using well-recorded media) can make your website stand out, and you more likely to be booked. A blog page is also effective for updating your current thoughts and comments on current news and for refreshing information for your site.

Your website should include multiple ways to contact you, including an e-mail address that you check regularly, a phone number, and a physical address. This contact information should remain the same wherever you use it online. Conflicting contact information can be confusing to a meeting planner or prospective client, and potentially the reason they don't choose you. You should also include your media kit on your site, and make sure it is available for download in a commonly used format—preferably a pdf.

Beyond your website, using social media can get your name and message in front of millions of online users around the world. However, it is important that you are putting yourself on the right sites and communicating the right messages, or you can hurt your credibility. When choosing social media sites, make sure you understand each site's purpose, its audience, and what features it employs.

You are likely familiar with the names of the "big three" social media outlets that have dominated the news over the past few years. Profiles on Facebook, LinkedIn, and Twitter are the basis of any speaker's or business's social media cloud (or network). Speakers may also want to use smaller but effective sites, such as Plaxo (business networking) and Naymz (reputation site). Other non-community-based sites, such as VisualCV, offer speakers a platform to present their background information, contact, and multimedia files.

When setting up your social media profiles, remember to be consistent. Use the same profile picture of you (not your logo) so you appear personable and approachable to your online peers. Be sure to double-check all of your dates and descriptions for employment and education. Meeting planners and potential clients looking for you online notice these sorts of discrepancies. Have a concise one-paragraph biography to post, as lengthy pages are harder to read and some sites limit your character count. If the site asks for a username to identify you by, use a professional-sounding name. Flirteegrl64 just wont get the same professional attention or following as RobinGSmithCSP.

Manage your social media message with microblogs. Microblogs are 140-character "sound bites" of information that are displayed on many social media sites (such as Facebook status messages) or are the main product of the site (such as Twitter). To use microblogs effectively to promote your speaking, you want your messages to be original, useful, valuable, fun, problem solving, and

Activity: Writing Effective Microblogs

Bad Microblog Examples

If you need an insurance plan, I have some openings in my schedule and can take on select clients. www.imaninsurer.com

Just had an interview today with a New York Times reporter. She was so rude!

Good Microblog Examples

Don't just anticipate your customer's future needs, create them! – www.burrus.com

Light blue & green colors provide the best energy in IT areas, hospitals, manufacturing, and deadline-oriented spaces. –www.patheydlauff.com

Write Your Own 140-Character Microblog

interesting. Your messages should be a welcome interlude for your followers, not an interruption. Whenever possible, end your microblogs with your website so readers are directed back to your main source of information.

To post messages responsibly for your speaking career, set up a schedule, and don't over-post. Over-posting can lead your readers to think you aren't actually working and can get you dropped from their list. Due to the ever-shifting nature of real-time search engine technology and other factors well beyond the average user's control, it is recommended that you post no more than once a day, and posting two to four times a week is a good level of activity. Remember that you are posting for your career as a speaker, not about personal issues like the fact your new puppy chewed your daughter's ballet shoe or that you are sooooooo tired. A good microblog is one that offers advice, solves an issue, and relays important information; it is not self-promotional.

LEVERAGE YOUR PUBLICITY INTO PROFITS

Now that you have published your great articles, been interviewed by reporters, and launched your online and social media efforts, what do you do? Use that publicity to get more business, that's what! All that effort wasn't just for fun; it was to position you to get more speaking engagements and higher-paid speaking engagements.

Put all of your new publicity efforts in your media kit. Your media kit is designed to tout you as an expert. All the publicity you get is evidence that each publication deems you to be an expert. Make sure everything significant to your career gets into your media kit.

Follow up with past clients and past almost clients. People you've worked with in the past are always the easiest to market to. They need to know every time you get published or quoted in an article. This keeps reestablishing your worth to them and makes you a valuable resource for their business.

Contact the association directors of the industries in whose trade publications your articles have been featured. Many publications are the journal of the trade association for that industry. If the editor felt that the membership was interested enough to print your article or interview you, then the executive director may be interested in hiring you to speak at one of their conferences.

Send a letter to the professional associations in the industries that have included you in their publications. If a publication isn't the association journal, you can still find the professional association for that industry and pitch them. Note that such-and-such magazine had recently published your article and you know this is a topic of interest to its members.

Send your updated information to speaker's bureaus or meeting planner services. Speaker's bureaus are in the business of promoting their clients. They promote with vigor those who are the easiest to get booked. Each bit of data you give them to pitch you to their clients makes you one of the easy ones. Meeting planners often also use online sites and services to find and book speakers.

The bottom line is that when you contact the right people with the right information, you could be on your way to a completely booked year.

Pam Lontos, MA, CSP, is president of PR/PR, a public relations firm that works with speakers, authors, and experts. She is the author of *I See Your Name Everywhere* and is a former vice president for Disney's Shamrock Broadcasting. PR/PR has placed clients in publications such as *USA Today, Entrepreneur, Time, Reader's Digest*, and *Cosmopolitan*. PR/PR works with established speakers, as well as those just launching their careers. For a free consultation, e-mail Pam@prpr.net or register at www.PRPR.net to receive *PR/PR Pulse!*—a free monthly e-newsletter.

A NICHE CAN MAKE YOU RICH

LeAnn Thieman, CSP, CPAE

When I quit my day job as a nurse and transitioned into a full-time professional speaker, I resisted advice to speak about health care. I didn't want to limit my message to a select few in a specific field. After all, my messages were universal and desperately needed by everyone in the United States, if not the entire world! Then, a National Speakers Association (NSA) mentor advised, "It's hard to send a marketing postcard to the entire world."

And he was right. Great speakers serve a niche, and doing so is the best way to start and to grow your business.

No matter your message or area of expertise, here's how to get started.

IDENTIFY YOUR NICHE.

Explore these questions:

- What past life experiences qualify you to speak?
- What educational background gives you expertise?
- What other educational courses have increased your knowledge and in what areas?
- What are you passionate about?
- What do you want to become an expert on?
- What do you know that will help others?
- What unique perspective can you bring?
- Who would trust what you have to say?

- In what industries are your current clients? Which hire you the most? Which are you most passionate about?

DIG DEEPER INTO YOUR NICHE.

Now that you have your messages organized and your niche identified, it's time to reach out to prospective audiences. Someone who specializes in health care can begin by contacting hospitals, nursing organizations, caregiver associations, and pharmaceutical companies, for example. Think about what an audience in your niche might look like.

- What organizations can you speak to in your chosen field?
- What organizations do your clients belong to? Your messages can likely be tailored for them, too.
- After speaking at one state association, send a testimonial letter to association chapters in other states.
- Ask the state association meeting planner to refer you to the national conference meeting planner.

BECOME THE EXPERT.

The best way to grow your business in a niche is to become the expert and understand the field from all angles. Although I knew a lot about nursing from 30 years at the bedside, I wasn't able to speak to chief nursing officers and human resource directors without learning more in all areas of the profession.

Determine what information you want to impart and what knowledge you're lacking, and then research, read, and take classes to become a well-respected authority on your topic.

- Read publications in your field of interest, e.g., periodicals, journals, books, and websites and other online articles and information (from credible sources).
- Talk to people in your industry at all levels, from CEOs to worker bees. Ask, "What are the three most important things I need to know?" and "What services and help do you need most?"
- Explore the NSA website, and research other speakers in your area of

expertise. What are they speaking on? What topics can you add that will set you apart? Who are their clients?

- Learn the lingo. Hopefully, your past experience in your field has already provided this knowledge. If not, it is crucial that you learn it. Do they refer to clients or customers? Patients or residents? CEOs or presidents?

- Learn their pain. (Yes, the adage is true: Find their pain and heal it.) What are their challenges? What does success look like to them?

- Join social media sites, and pay attention to conversations and questions to learn hot topics and current information in your niche.

- Learn to use Google Alerts (or similar searches) to receive niche-related Internet articles.

CRAFT AND PERFECT YOUR KEYNOTE OR TRAINING SESSIONS.

Once you've established the pearls of wisdom and life-changing lessons you want to share, it's time to craft a knock-their-socks-off keynote. This is a time to utilize NSA's resources and even consider hiring a coach.

Using your specialized knowledge, research, and expertise, write or revamp your keynote or training specifically for your niche market. Remember, your message should be what they need to hear, not just what you want to say.

DESIGN PROMOTIONAL MATERIALS FOR YOUR NICHE.

If your current one-sheet is generic (targeted toward the whole world), it's time to rewrite it with messages that are targeted specifically to your niche.

You've researched your target audience's pain. Your marketing materials are an opportunity to let them know you can help heal it.

- Tap into NSA workshops, CDs, and conferences to learn how to list the benefits of your presentations, as they apply to your specific niche.

- Create or re-craft promotional materials and a website with this information. Remember to clearly state not just how great you are but also the benefits you offer.

- Create other materials and website pages for specialty areas within your niche. For example, if your expertise is in goal setting, you might have materials aimed at women, another set for corporate executives, another for small business owners, etc.

BUILD A DATABASE OF POTENTIAL CLIENTS WHO NEED YOUR MESSAGE.

- Buy a contact management database, such as ACT! or Goldmine.
- Purchase the National Trade and Professional Associations (NTPA) book or CD. This is available at the library, but buying your own copy lets you mark it up and get the most out of it. This resource lists every association in the United States, with current contact information, conference dates, annual budgets, and much more. Find the areas that fit your selected niche. For example, a nursing expert might look into nursing organizations, health care associations, and medical associations, among others. Identify the top 300 or so, then enter each into your database.
- Search the Internet for organizations and associations in your field.
- Include organizations and associations mentioned in the niche-related periodicals you are reading, as well as online white papers and articles.
- Read ads in the periodicals and websites you study. What companies, corporations, or institutions place ads? They are trying to reach the same audience you are and may have conferences and a need for speakers.
- Ask your clients what associations they belong to.
- Consider purchasing a database specific to your niche.

If you are a beginning speaker, limit your initial database to 300 to 500 to keep it manageable, because next you need to call them. That's right, call them!

CONTACT YOUR POTENTIAL CLIENTS.

- Call a minimum of 10 potential clients per day and you can complete your initial database in about a month. The truth is, you can call 10 in an hour, because these days, you'll probably leave phone messages about 80 percent of the time. Your message should be succinct and benefit-driven, explaining what you offer and asking what their needs are and how you may serve. Tell them to watch for an e-mail with _____ (your message) in the subject line.

- Send an e-mail overview of what you offer, then inquire again about their needs and challenges and how you can help them.

- Six to eight weeks later, send them something in the mail—a marketing postcard, flyer, or one-sheet. Remember, it takes an average of seven contacts before they book you.

- "Drip" on your prospective clients at least four times a year. Call them or e-mail them an article you've written. Mail them a postcard announcing your newest presentation. Be on the forefront of their minds when they are ready to make a decision.

- Offer to speak for free or at a reduced fee if an event will put you in front of decision makers—those who can hire you—in your niche. In your contract, state in-kind services you request in lieu of your full fee. Those might include a testimonial letter, an introduction to three other potential clients, a membership list, the contact information of all attendees, an article in their publications, an ad in their magazine or journal, and/or professional videotaping of your presentation.

- Send press releases to prospects, clients, and meeting planners with new information, your spectacular accomplishments, etc.

AT THE EVENT

One of the best ways to increase your expertise and delve deep into your niche is to be a stellar presenter.

- Prior to the event, do your homework by learning as much about the client as possible. Send a pre-program questionnaire to learn their goals and expectations of your presentation(s). Ask, "What would make it a 10?" From the client's website, learn their mission statement, company goals, etc.

- Arrive early and stay late. Spend time with your client the evening before or throughout the event. Ask questions. Listen. Learn about them and the industry.

- On your session evaluation form, ask questions such as "What was most helpful?" and "What else would you like to learn about?" These questions help you to learn their needs, hone your message, and increase your expertise.

- On your evaluation ask, "What other organizations do you know that could benefit from my message?"

- Finally, ask them this important question: "What are you going to do differently after hearing today's presentation?" This is where you identify the real benefit of your message. Ask, "May I quote you?" These testimonials are invaluable to share with future clients and include on your marketing materials.

- During your presentation, drop subtle hints of other topics you offer and those you serve. "When I was doing ABC for XYZ, I learned . . ."

- Offer additional services in areas where you are experienced, such as doing a round table discussion, facilitation, emceeing the event, doing a survey, etc.

- Have products conveying your messages for sale after the event. Your content should be so great they want to learn more and share it at home and work.

AFTER THE EVENT

- Call the client for a post-event conference call (arranged before the event.) Ask some of the same questions from your evaluation form, then add, "Most of my business comes from client referrals. Can you suggest others you know who could benefit from my message?" Ask them to make the call or e-mail of introduction. If not, contact the potential client, mentioning the event you did with his or her colleague.

- Add contacts from the written evaluations to your database and—you guessed it—contact them soon, deepening your niche.

- When attendees give you their business cards, call or e-mail them within a week after the event, asking how you can serve. Too many speakers miss these great warm leads while searching for cold ones.

- If you received the list of attendees, add them to your database, and then send them an e-mail within a few weeks to share a tip or reinforce your message.

- Get a testimonial letter stating not that you are a fabulous speaker, but what the attendees learned from your presentation and how they benefited. (You may even consider adding this to your contract to ensure compliance.)

WRITE FOR YOUR NICHE MARKET.

Send informative articles to the journals, magazines, and websites your prospects and clients read.

- Check the website or periodical for guidelines. Follow them exactly. If the editor's name is not listed, call to find it, as those without a name are discarded. Few journals pay for freelance articles, so offer them at no cost if your brief bio will appear at the end, stating your area of expertise, your website, and contact information.
- Write for a compilation book in your niche. There are established companies that offer this opportunity. Connect with other experts in your field (many from NSA), and write your own compilation book.
- Write white papers with expert content. Share with (or sell to) prospects and clients.
- When, and only when, you've become an expert, write a book specifically to serve your niche. This reinforces your lessons and adds to back-of-room sales.

Following these tips will help you delve deep into your niche, and you will grow rich . . . with opportunities to serve, sharing your expertise with the world.

LeAnn Thieman, CSP, CPAE, began her speaking career by sharing life-balance lessons from her daring adventure of rescuing orphans at the end of the Vietnam War. A professional speaker for 15 years and now a member of the Speaker Hall of Fame, she serves health care associations and organizations, hospitals, foundations, and woman's organizations. LeAnn has written 12 *Chicken Soup for the Soul* books, plus *Balancing Life in Your "War Zones": A Guide to Physical, Mental and Spiritual Health.* She is a regular columnist for several journals, magazines, and websites in her health care niche.

TELL THE RIGHT STORY AT THE RIGHT TIME

Bruce Hale

Stories are a speaker's best friend. There's a relaxing—a leaning-in—that occurs when listeners realize you've begun to tell a tale and, during that storytelling, a bond forms between speaker and audience.

Stories connect. And what's more, stories stick. Six months later, a listener may have completely forgotten your "12 Keys of Sensational Selling," but she'll remember your account of your first disastrous sales call.

The human brain is wired to seek out stories—a remnant of our primitive past, when remembering a hunter's tale about which cave to avoid could help guarantee living to hunt another day. Stories also engage the emotions. If you want to inspire listeners and want them to remember you (and rehire you), stories are the key.

But not just any random tale will do. To truly be effective, you must tell the right story at the right time.

The saga of your lost weekend in Las Vegas may be a hit with a college audience, but not such a good fit for a group of bankers. Likewise, a folktale may provide a perfect metaphor in your corporate presentation, but leave a crowd of nurses unmoved.

So, how do you know which tale suits which occasion? And once you've identified it, how do you tell it effectively?

THE FIVE ESSENTIAL TYPES OF TALES

You'll find a wide variety of story types out there—everything from the archetypal

Hero's Journey to the apocryphal (and overdone) Starfish Story. Although each has its place, five types of tales are indispensable for speakers.

The Signature Story

Have you ever sat in the audience and marveled at a speaker's story, a tale that was intensely personal and yet universal? That's a signature story and, in many cases, it can serve as the foundation of a presentation. Signature stories tend to be longer and full of detail. (If you don't yet have one, use the processes in the "Your Life" section on page 177 to unearth yours.)

One of my own signature stories involves the time I foolishly volunteered to play Elvis and performed a parody song at a nonprofit's fundraiser—after being away from the stage for 17 years. The story is personal and specific to me. Yet I've heard from audience members years later that its catchphrase became a catchphrase in their own family. That's universal.

The "Why I'm Here" Story

This helps you make an emotional connection with the listener, and it can be told one-on-one or in a group. Distinct from the signature story, the why-I'm-here story should be a brief one. It helps sell you to your listeners, and lets them know, in essence, who you are.

For example, an acquaintance was getting ready to dump her financial advisor, who had terrible people skills. When my exasperated friend asked the advisor, "Why are you doing this job anyway?" she got a story in response. The advisor revealed that she'd been raised by a single mother, living hand-to-mouth, and that when she grew up, she vowed to do whatever she could to keep other women from undergoing that same trauma.

My friend stayed with the advisor.

The Elephant in the Room Story

If you know your audience is thinking or feeling something that they're not expressing, you can address their concerns in a nonconfrontational way with a story. Often, this can disarm listeners and shift their perspective—or at least let them know you understand their concerns.

I heard a tale about a young hotshot CEO who was going to speak at his first board meeting, to a board composed of grizzled industry veterans. He knew they'd be skeptical about his abilities and attitude. So, he told the tale of how he once ignored advice when getting his yacht ready to sail, and what he learned from that. The story helped start their new relationship on an even keel (so to speak).

The Success Story

This is a short story or case study that helps establish your bona fides. Generally, it's a tale of how someone used your product or service, and how it helped him or her solve a problem. This type of story can be used one-on-one, in meetings, and with audiences.

In my own talks, I sometimes tell how I consulted with a city councilman on his reelection campaign, helping him choose and refine stories to address key issues. He went on to win reelection. While I wish I could claim *all* of the credit for that, there's no doubt that his improved storytelling helped.

The Example Story

This can serve to punctuate a key point in your presentation. Generally, you'll want to keep your example stories short and sweet, especially if you've got a lot of points to cover. The tale can occur before or after the learning point, and it can be positive or negative, depending upon the effect you seek.

In my presentations, I make a point about the importance of understanding your listener before telling your tale. In my example story, a financial advisor loses his client by recommending she invest heavily in Japanese stocks—not having bothered to learn that the woman lost her husband in WWII to a Japanese bomb. The story is negative, but it makes the point.

WHERE TO FIND TALES TO TELL

So, now you know what type of tale you want to tell in your presentation. The next step is locating the right story of that type.

My own bias leans toward true personal anecdotes. After all, you know them intimately, and it's hard for listeners to argue with something that actually happened. But they're not always the best story for the job—moreover, your life experience may not have given you the story you need for that particular presentation.

Before settling on your tale, be sure to explore all avenues of story sources. Here are three major sources for stories, along with some resources to get you started:

1. Myths and Folktales

These are usually best suited to a formal speech, where they can be used to establish a metaphor that you refer to repeatedly. But they also can work in training sessions, if the folktale is brief and appropriate.

Here's an example of folktale-as-metaphor: Back when I was working as a corporate speechwriter in Hawaii, one CEO found himself needing to "rally the troops." I had him tell the legend of Maui and his brothers fishing the Hawaiian Islands from the ocean, and drew from it a lesson on the power of teamwork that we wove throughout his speech.

Similarly, you might pick a tale of Mullah Nasrudin, the "wise fool" of Sufism, to make a point about how a company might be misinterpreting its challenges.

One caveat: Be sure you pick a tale that works for your telling style. For example, if you're uncomfortable doing character voices, don't pick a story that relies heavily on a perfect Scottish brogue. (Unless, of course, you're Scottish.)

Here are some resources to help you in your story quest:

Three-Minute Tales, by Margaret Read MacDonald

Nasrudin, by Idries Shah

Favorite Folktales from Around the World, edited by Jane Yolen

Tim Sheppard's Storytelling Resources for Storytellers (website): www.timsheppard.co.uk/story/tellinglinks.html#How%20to%20Tell%20Stories

National Storytelling Network's Resources Page (website): www.storynet.org/Resources/LinksList/index.html

2. OPS (Other People's Stories)

OPS are particularly effective in small groups but can work in any speaking situation. Keep your ears and eyes open, and you'll find these stories all around you—on the radio, in casual conversation, online, or in print. (The *Chicken Soup for the Soul* series is an excellent source for inspirational OPS.)

Aside from conducting a Google search for "stories about integrity" or some such, you can also poll your friends, family, and coworkers for anecdotes on your topic.

Ask them questions like:

- Do you remember a time when the issue of ___ came up?
- Was there a time when you had to make a difficult choice?
- Can you recall a time when you faced a challenge and prevailed?
- Tell me about a breakthrough experience you've had.
- What's the best customer service story you've ever heard?

If you're speaking at a corporation or association, don't miss the chance to collect some of the group's stories and use them in your talk. Ask some key stakeholders for a story that best exemplifies the company's mission, for example, or expresses a critical problem facing the organization. When you use this story in your speech, your listeners will feel like you really "get" them.

3. Your Life

By far, your own life is the richest source of anecdotes and stories for all occasions. This is where you'll find your why-I'm-here tale and your signature story. Your life is also an excellent source for "values" stories that convey a belief you're trying to communicate to the group.

For example, if I wanted to tell a story that touched on honesty, I might tell about the time I shoplifted some bubblegum, my dad caught me, and I had what some call a "learning experience." (Others call it not being able to sit down for a week.)

You can mine the rich vein of your life's stories in several ways:

Mind-mapping: On a big sheet of paper, write the chief characteristic of the story you're trying to elicit, say, "risk-taking." Circle it, and draw many lines radiating from the circle, like the rays of the sun. As fast as possible, jot words or phrases along those lines—the first things that come to mind. Often, stories will be connected with the words you free-associate.

Ask yourself questions:

- When in my life was I scared/happy/surprised/etc.? Often, good stories have a strong emotion attached to them.

- When was I faced with a difficult choice, and what did I learn from that?

- What peak or breakthrough experiences have I had in my life?

Remember your firsts: Often, your first experiences come with a vivid story everyone can relate to. Make a list of as many firsts as you can—first kiss, first job, first fender-bender, first arrest—and jot down the key points of the stories that follow.

Also, you can create a timeline of your life, broken into ten-year chunks. For each period, see if you can recall a handful of peak experiences relating to different aspects of your life—family, work, play, spirituality, learning. Some of the stories may not have a point, but you might unearth some gems.

Check out these esources:

- NSA member Craig Harrison's "The Speaker As Storyteller" and "Homegrown Humor" handouts at: http://www. expressionsofexcellence.com/nsa.html

- NSA's Storytellers PEG (Professional Emphasis Group) holds monthly teleseminars on storytelling topics.

BEFORE YOU TELL THE STORY . . .

Finally, no matter where you find potential stories, run them through the relevance test before investing the time to learn them. Make sure they serve the purpose you intend. And make sure you've chosen the right story for your situation.

What makes a story "right"? Here are nine key concepts to consider in making that determination:

1. **Brief is better.** Choose a story that can be boiled down to two to three minutes, if possible. Lengthier tales can get too complex for a business setting. Remember, a good story should be like a skirt: long enough to cover the subject, but short enough to keep things interesting.

2. **What is the *Why*?** Why are you telling this particular story? Make sure

it reinforces the point you want to make, with no ambiguity. Knowing the key point of your story will help you choose what to leave in and what to leave out. It will also help you craft a bridge line that ties your story back into your speech.

3. **This time, it's personal.** Find a story from your own life, if possible—especially for a why-I'm-here tale. Personal stories lend you authority and authenticity.

4. **Who's your hero?** Listeners need a clear protagonist to identify with. If you have too many heroes, the tale and the audience both lose focus. Telling your story from a single main character's point of view keeps things streamlined, plain, and powerful.

5. **What's the beef?** Every story needs a clear problem and solution. Make sure this problem is relevant to your listeners, and remember to include the solution. Listeners need closure.

6. **Make 'em feel it.** If you want your story to hit home, pick one with strong human emotion. Fear, anger, excitement, frustration, joy—it doesn't matter which feeling, as long as it's genuine. Your involvement in the story's emotion triggers your listeners' emotional involvement.

7. **Keep it real.** For most business purposes, true stories resonate more than parables or myths. *Who Moved My Cheese?* aside, would you relate better to a story that happened to the teller or one that happened to mice?

8. **All's well that ends well.** Where you can, pick a story with a happy ending. Why? It'll give your listeners an endorphin rush and leave them with a positive impression. Yes, fear can motivate, but it can also lead to paralysis. Take a tip from Hollywood and end on an up note.

9. **Papa, don't preach.** At your story's end, let the listeners draw their own conclusions. If you spell out the moral in letters 10-feet high, you ram it down their throats. Leave some space for the audience to reach its own conclusions, and you draw people in.

It's a funny thing about storytelling—the more you do it, the better you get. Practice stories on your family, your spouse, your dog. Spend some time listening to the masters in the field, whether it's Garrison Keillor, your Aunt Fran, or one of the many superlative storytellers in NSA. Learn their techniques, and then go beyond those techniques.

Ultimately, what makes a good storyteller is a unique voice. If you take the time to develop yours, through practice, experimentation, and repetition, your distinct style will emerge in time.

Everybody has a story to tell, and the world needs *your* stories.

An award-winning author and speaker, Bruce Hale is a Fulbright Scholar in storytelling, who studied the folklore of Thailand. He blends his experience as a corporate communicator with his acting and storytelling training to help business people and organizations across the United States reach their goals through super-charged communication. Visit www.brucetalks.com.

HOW TO WRITE A COMPELLING
BOOK PROPOSAL

Barbara Glanz, CSP

One of the ongoing debates for professional speakers is whether to self-publish or to go the mainstream publishing route. The reality is, speakers can make money and increase their visibility either way. In recent years, technology and pricing have made the former an attractive option for many speakers. Many authors, and I count myself among them, still swear by the credibility, marketing, distribution, and other benefits of the latter. While traditional publishing can seem like a daunting task, here are seven tips that can simplify the process to becoming an author.

Tip 1: Always be thinking of how you can leverage the material you already have.

My first book, *The Creative Communicator—399 Ways to Communicate Commitment Without Boring People to Death,* started out as a 16-page booklet I compiled as a handout for a speech. As I was working on the booklet, I decided that the whole concept could be expanded into a book idea with a bit of extra effort rather than starting something on another topic from scratch.

Tip 2: Always make friends with gatekeepers and use names of mutual contacts.

I had heard many good things about Irwin Professional Publishing, a Chicago area publisher that was also a Times Mirror company. After researching the name of the senior editor of its business book division, I called him, did a little name-dropping, and shared my idea with him. Although he was surprised that I got through, he had a good sense of humor and liked my idea. After sending a creative written proposal and several meetings, I had a check and a contract.

Tip 3: Always make friends with as many people in the publishing company as possible.

The average business book sells 3,000 copies, and I surpassed that mark. Because the book had sold well, another division of the company called and asked me if I would do a book for their new Business Skills Express series. Thus, after a written proposal and some negotiation, *Building Customer Loyalty—How YOU Can Help Keep Customers Returning* was born. One of the reasons this opportunity came about was that I had made a concerted effort to get to know as many people as I could at Irwin. I offered to speak to the whole company on the topic of my first book, and helped them implement some of the ideas to improve their communication and customer service. Visibility and good relationships not only encourage a publisher to sell books, it helps keep authors at top of mind for future projects.

Tip 4: Network with anyone, anywhere . . . because anything can happen!

When I began formulating the idea for my "heart" book, *CARE Packages for the Workplace—Dozens of Little Things You Can Do to Regenerate Spirit at Work*, I shared my concept with a woman I met in the ladies' washroom at a convention in Anaheim, California. She offered an introduction to her boss, who she said was interested in the topic.

When I returned to my room that evening, there was a message from her saying that she and her boss wanted to have lunch with me the next afternoon. That "boss" turned out to be renowned author and management expert Ken Blanchard! Not only did he use the signature story to close his speech, but he also called several weeks later and asked if he could write the foreword to the book because of his belief in the topic. (It was also proof of the power of having an unforgettable experience or story to exemplify a book's message. Readers—and editors—will never forget a story!)

Tip 5: Add something creative to your proposal to get the editor's attention.

With this book, I wanted to pursue an even bigger publisher. In discussions with friends who were authors, the same company and same editor's name kept coming up. I called him and shared my idea, and he asked for a proposal.

Because the whole book idea was based on the acronym and metaphor of CARE packages, I included in the proposal several 1" by 2" brown cardboard boxes with the letters "CARE" and my name and number stamped on them—just like packages sent during World War II. My intention was to give one of these to every audience member at presentations. The publisher expanded the idea by giving them out at the introductory sales conference and having salespeople distribute them at bookstores.

Tip 6: Study proposals that sold books.

It can be frustrating to send out 30 or 40 proposals, and some tactics may sound "too easy to be true." But success comes down to a couple of factors: pre-research; networking; solid, marketable ideas; and dynamite proposals. *Write the Perfect Book Proposal,* by Jeff Herman and Deborah M. Adams, gives an excellent overview, including the common elements of winning book proposals.

The two most important sections are "Competition" and "Promotion." Publishers love speakers. Many are willing to negotiate above the customary 40 percent discount for speakers who purchase a certain number of books in the first year. Speakers can help assure the publisher that marketing and selling is a priority, by documenting the number of annual presentations; client lists; published articles and interviews; creative marketing ideas; spin-off product possibilities; and media contacts. Donating a portion of royalties to a nonprofit organization (as I did with CARE) adds a dimension of giving back and can even facilitate extras such as permission to promote with their copyrighted name.

Tip 7: Take note of publishing companies in similar topic areas.

Bookstores and catalogues are an essential part of determining the competition—and deciding how a book will be different from what is already out there. There are countless ideas that real organizations are using in their workplaces to stimulate creativity and commitment in readers—and they are a critical part of any proposal. A great idea that is a little (or a lot) different, on a topic that is of vital interest to a particular market, has a great chance of being picked up by a publisher.

Above all, the speaker-turned-author needs passion. It's a matter of believing the message and authenticating it through every aspect of life and work. An editor who detects passion and commitment to a distinctive, marketable idea will be eager to create and sign a contract—it's an editor's job to find good material and bring it to market. A great idea, honed by research and networking and formulated into a knock-their-socks off proposal, will be too much to resist.

Book Proposal Structure—Required Sections

BOOK CONCEPT

This overview describes the book in succinct, objective terms. The "what" covers the primary concept and scope of the book. The "why" gives the background of what's happening in the marketplace that creates the need for the book. Specify the length of the manuscript in words, describe illustrations and/or photographs, and give projected date of completion. 1-2 pages.

PURPOSE

States the main purpose or theme of the book in one or two sentences. This is a sound bite that would impress the media as well as a publisher.

MARKET

Describes, in detail, the audience for the book—even the number of potential buyers. Needs to be as specific as possible and avoid broad generalizations. 1 page.

COMPETITION

Lists competitive books and states how this book is different and better, without being overly critical of other books. The key is to answer the question: "Why should there be another book on the market?" 1-2 pages.

CONTENT SUMMARY

Provides a table of contents for at least 10 chapters, using titles and subtitles. The titles should be informal or catchy and the subtitles descriptive. They are key selling points and can be a make-or-break part of retail book sales. 1-2 pages.

CHAPTER SUMMARIES

Gives a short summary of each chapter. One or two paragraphs (1/4 to 1/2 page), or as long as a page. Many publishers will want a sample chapter or two to demonstrate writing style. 3-10 pages.

AUTHOR

Provides qualifications and experience. List previous publications and advantages, such as industry contacts, resources, research data, personal experiences, etc., that would indicate influence and ability to sell books. Usually 1 page.

PROMOTION

Lists all means and factors that will assist the publisher in promoting and selling the book. Examples are workshops or classes, making presentations at regional and national conventions, writing magazine or journal articles, appearing on radio or TV, etc. Usually 1 page.

OPTIONAL SECTIONS:

Comments from Readers

If others, particularly well-known names from leading organizations, have read the proposal and have favorable comments, their comments may be good selling points. This section should read like book jacket copy. Speaker contacts and clients who are willing to provide a testimonial for the book when completed can be included here. Usually 1-2 pages.

Research Methodology

For research-based topics, this section expands on the techniques and methods. New research can be a powerful selling point.

Sample of Writing

Short, recently published articles (especially those that cover the same topic) can be included as a sample of writing style.

Supportive Material

Short newspaper or magazine clippings, describing market factors that create a need for the book, can be good selling points.

ADDITIONAL RESOURCES

Books and Articles

How to Write a Book Proposal—Michael Larsen, Writer's Digest Books
Write the Perfect Book Proposal—Jeff Herman and Deborah M. Adams
How to Get Happily Published—Judith Appelbaum
"How to Write an Irresistible Book Proposal," Bud Gardner, *Professional Speaker* magazine, July 1994
Books in Print

The Writer's Market
Publisher's Weekly
Literary Market Place
NSA Directory of Learning Resources

Suggested Conferences and Workshops

Publisher's University sponsored by Publishers Marketing Association, 310-372-2732

Barbara Glanz, CSP, works with organizations that want to improve morale, retention, and service and with people who want to rediscover the joy in their work and in their lives. Barbara has presented on all seven continents and in all 50 states since 1995. She is the author of *The Simple Truths of Service Inspired by Johnny the Bagger; The Simple Truths of Appreciation—How Each of Us Can Choose to Make a Difference; 180 Ways to Spread Contagious Enthusiasm; Balancing Acts; CARE Packages for Your Customers; Handle with CARE—Motivating and Retaining Employees; CARE Packages for the Workplace—Dozens of Little Things You Can Do to Regenerate Spirit at Work; CARE Packages for the Home; What Can I Do? Ideas to Help Those Who Have Experienced Loss; Building Customer Loyalty;* and *The Creative Communicator.* For more information, e-mail her at bglanz@barbaraglanz.com or visit www.barbaraglanz.com.

SEVEN STRATEGIES TO GUIDE YOU THROUGH THE VIRTUAL WORLD

Susan Friedmann, CSP, and Gina Schreck, CSP

You've always enjoyed the process of speaking: putting on your power suit, pulling together your materials and props, and standing in front of a roomful of people. Somehow, sitting at your computer and speaking to people who are at their computers, too, just isn't the same, is it? But whether you like it or not, virtual events are gaining in popularity, and that means savvy speakers can't ignore them.

The rise of virtual conferences and webinars does not signal the demise of live events, but many companies are experimenting with virtual counterparts to supplement or augment face-to-face meetings and conferences, as well as to provide ongoing content, follow-up opportunities, and a deeper reach into certain market segments.

The 2010 *Virtual Market Outlook Report (VMOR)* released by the Event Marketing Institute noted, "The market is still figuring out the full potential of virtual and how best to harness its power. In the face of economic uncertainty and driven by the need to constantly refresh how brands and audiences connect with one another, virtual is a bigger part of the conversation than ever before."

Wired magazine predicted that we'd see a 500 percent increase in virtual events in 2010. And GigaOm.com, a highly regarded technology website, predicts that high-end virtual technology and virtual worlds will grow from approximately $50 million in 2009 to $8 billion to $10 billion by 2014.

In other words, the meeting industry landscape is changing dramatically, and speakers need to adapt.

It might look as though virtual events just appeared out of nowhere. But they have been around for more than ten years. The early primitive versions used very basic technology that needed considerable bandwidth for anyone to participate adequately. Ten years ago, bandwidth was considerably slower and more expensive than today. But virtual events have come a long way over the past several years, evolving from cartoonish environments to streamlined 3D cyber-venues. The technology is now very affordable and continues to advance by leaps and bounds. This means that staying current and learning how to use this powerful new marketing tool can pose a challenge to the professional speaker.

THE SPEAKER'S CHALLENGE

Using virtual events platforms effectively—and with confidence—can be a challenge. It requires a new set of skills that clients expect you to have ready so that you can easily and effortlessly participate in their online events.

For many speakers, as with most people, a lack of knowledge of the unknown often leads to intimidation, fear, and anxiety. Because it frequently takes time to grasp new technology and to understand its applications, whether for business or everyday use, it's easy to employ the "busyness" excuse to shy away until it becomes absolutely necessary to learn it.

Virtual events often fall into this category. Plus, they add a level of resistance for speakers who view them as impersonal and complicated. Some feel that not being in the same room with the audience makes it difficult or even impossible to make a real impact and connection.

But once you know and understand how this new tool can boost your business, you'll likely embrace and use it—especially when it speaks to your bottom line. Virtual events give you that opportunity because you can now reach people and places you previously never thought possible.

Virtual events also add a deeper dimension to your business model, incorporating sustainability and globalization. For example, when you leave a face-to-face event, you may easily be forgotten. However, your virtual events, when recorded, can take on a life (and revenue stream) all their own.

To help you better understand the virtual event environment, the following seven strategies are designed to show you how this powerful and exciting tool can give your business a boost.

STRATEGY #1: UNDERSTAND THE BASICS.

What exactly is meant by *virtual*? A virtual event is a gathering of many people connected through a common online environment.

- A *virtual event* could be a trade show, webcast, online job fair, conference, or other similar event.

- A *virtual environment* is a computer-hosted, simulated environment, such as Second Life, Teleplace, Protosphere, and other 3D immersive environments.

- A *web or virtual meeting* is an online meeting tool for planning, preparation, training, coaching, or desktop information sharing. (Source: *2010 Virtual Meeting Outlook Report*)

In addition to the above, you are likely to come across some of the following terms:

- A *hybrid event* refers to a physical and virtual component held simultaneously or in some combination. This provides a significant solution for remote employees or attendees who unable to attend in person.

- *Simulcasting,* or *simultaneous broadcasting,* refers to a program or event broadcast at the same time over one or more mediums. For example, the Metropolitan Opera in New York recently introduced simulcasting of a selection of their live events to be viewed in remote locations, domestically and internationally.

- A *webcast* is Internet broadcasting. The technology provides streaming video of lectures in universities, speeches at conferences, and a wide variety of other events.

- A *webinar* is a Web-based seminar, commonly known as online workshops. Many companies offer webinars as an alternative to traditional learning environments.

How Are Organizations Using Virtual Events?

As organizations look to adopt the virtual environment into their meeting and event strategy, they have three options—to *supplement*, *complement*, or *replace* their physical counterparts.

According to VMOR's research study of 889 marketers, "the most popular use of virtual technology is for presentations (61 percent), internal meetings (56 percent), training and education (53 percent)—typically delivered via webcasts and webinars, followed by more robust solutions, conferences (48 percent), and trade shows (32 percent)."

Microsoft, Amazon, Cisco, Accenture, and others hold career fairs with keynote and breakout sessions in 3D cyberspaces. Manpower Staffing has an entire campus in Second Life dedicated to recruiting talent and providing career search programs.

STRATEGY #2: SNAG SPEAKER OPPORTUNITIES.

Meeting planners look to speakers to provide insights, awareness, and new information, whether live or virtual. That's why speakers need to understand the virtual technology enough to make valuable suggestions and offer strategic solutions. For example, if timing isn't right for a live event, a speaker could urge the meeting planner to host a virtual meeting. Consider this: A trade show organizer recently wanted to set up an exhibitor training program just prior to the start of the show. But for exhibitors, who have various pre-show responsibilities, attending a live training program interferes with those important activities. So, as a solution, the organizer held a virtual meeting several weeks beforehand. The meeting allowed exhibitors to learn the before-, during-, and after-the-show essentials without cutting into their set up, networking, and prep time—a far better use of their time and resources.,

Whether your clients supplement, complement, or replace their in-person meetings with virtual counterparts, these extra events offer speakers multiple opportunities to sell their services. Plus, virtual events provide longevity. Once over, the meeting can live on the organizer's website for extended periods, giving your words of wisdom a greater life span and reach.

HIMSS (Healthcare Information & Management Systems Society) organizes virtual conferences in addition to MedTech, its major in-person trade show. The live show draws nearly 30,000 people; however, HIMSS discovered its virtual events didn't compete with their physical equivalent. In a survey conducted after the event, between 70 percent and 80 percent of the virtual attendees never attended the physical event even before HIMSS offered the virtual option.

STRATEGY #3: LEARN HOW TO ADAPT YOUR SPEAKING STYLE.

At a recent virtual event, a Disney representative voiced his dilemma of finding speakers and trainers with virtual experience. He referred to the lack of this experience as one of his greatest challenges in putting on successful events.

Motivational speakers rely heavily on the energy and dynamics of live interaction. This atmosphere changes dramatically in the virtual environment. Equivalent to a radio interview, you often find yourself talking into thin air. Your energy-motivator lifeline no longer exists. Your face-to-face audience now consists of other avatars, or perhaps just your dog, cat, or goldfish. And no matter how much you adore your pets, they simply are no substitute for the dynamism of a live audience.

This means that to work virtually, adapting your speaking style to the technology is essential. In the same way you would adopt a different delivery style when presenting to a group of ten, versus an army of thousands, you need different skills. Does this mean you can't share your inspirational message virtually? Absolutely not! You just need to modify your tempo to the environment. However, to sound engaging as you talk to your computer screen is most definitely a practiced art.

In addition, keynote speakers who resist using presentation software, such as PowerPoint or Keynote, will find that these are essential tools along with others that you may need to help convey your message virtually.

STRATEGY #4: GET STARTED.

In the current tight economy, you may well find that many of your clients are turning to the virtual environment to save money with their meetings and events. This means that there's no time like the present to dip your toe in the water and get started learning and practicing the skills you need to add virtual presentations to your service offerings.

Given the plethora of webinars and virtual offerings currently available on the Internet, chances are you've already attended at least one, such as those organized by NSA University.

The 3-Step Process

Attending an event is step one in a three-step "getting started" process. Find events where you can participate and observe. Log in to learn, whether on a webinar, attending a networking event, or signing in for a class in a 3D virtual world, like Teleplace or Second Life.

The second step is to present your own program material through services such as Business Expert Webinars and Copper Conferencing. These services arrange and market the event for you so that you can focus on your presentation.

The third and final step is to organize your own program, using services such as GotoWebinar, Adobe Connect, or Elluminate. As with everything you do, practice makes perfect.

Once you feel confident presenting in the virtual world, it's time to let your clients know you're all set to participate in their virtual meetings.

STRATEGY #5: GET CREATIVE WITH FEES.

With the tight economy, you're all too familiar with budget cuts, which force many of your clients to eliminate or cut back on hiring speakers. Appearing virtually saves everyone time and money, and it provides the convenience of connecting experts with those seeking the information.

Imagine: no travel hassles, you show up online at the appointed time, present your material for 60 to 90 minutes; then you're done and can enjoy a home-cooked meal with family or friends. Obviously, you still have preparation and follow-up activities with the client and/or audience participants. You can also offer a follow-up virtual event to your face-to-face events with little or no additional cost, allowing you to maintain or raise your fees. Not having to leave your home office when you present virtually provides an extra bonus, never mind that you can do more virtual events in one day than you can in person. With this type of convenience, it's worth incorporating a more flexible fee structure to appear virtually, especially when you could exceed your daily or per-event fee.

STRATEGY #6: START THINKING SMALLER.

When you approach your business as a content provider, rather than just a speaker, it's easier to envision the multiple platforms where you can offer your content to those seeking it. Virtually, you have the opportunity to deliver your content using different tools. If you currently conduct longer programs—several hours, days, or weeks—you'll have to break your material into smaller chunks to deliver it in multiple sittings.

As you look through your content, start thinking in byte-sized pieces. For example, can you deliver a face-to-face session and follow up with virtual coaching? Can you deliver three 90-minute sessions, instead of an all-day speaking or training event? Can you provide homework to allow participants to begin applying the new skills, and then start your next session with success stories or group sharing?

What about creating video pieces to introduce your participants to a particular topic before you hold a webinar or hosting a live video-streamed follow-up session to answer more questions a week after your initial presentation? The possibilities are endless.

STRATEGY #7: UNDERSTAND THE CONSEQUENCES.

Naturally, deciding not to be a part of the virtual world is an option. However, before making any rash and final decisions on the subject, it's important to know and understand the consequences.

The greatest consequence is possible extinction as you lose your market share to savvy new, and perhaps younger, competitors hungry and eager for action. The rising Gen Xers in the marketplace embrace the technology that many baby boomers find intimidating and want to avoid. Many of them see the opportunities and recognize the need to establish themselves as virtual speakers.

Those under the age of 35 are native to this technology and gravitate to it naturally. It doesn't mean they like it, but they have grown up in the age of video games and online communities. Those older than 35 are emigrating into this digital landscape a few at a time—some embracing it with a sense of adventure, some coming along griping, kicking, and screaming—and of course, there are those who refuse to leave their comfortable, yet emptier, homesteads.

The bottom line is . . . well, your bottom line. The more you get in tune with virtual events and what they can do for you, and more importantly, for your business, the better off you'll be. The technology is here to stay, and it's constantly changing, improving, and being made available to greater numbers of people. The question is: Will you embrace it, or will you ignore it?

Take time to get to know and understand what being a part of the virtual world can do for you. Start small, but start. Choose one new virtual delivery platform or tool for a month. Dive in, learn as much as you can, then play and have fun. The more you know, the less it will intimidate you. In fact, quite the opposite! You might even develop an affinity for the technology you once avoided. As Susan Jeffers's book title goes, "Feel the fear and do it anyway." You just might discover a whole new world of opportunities that can take your speaking business to greater profitability. The sky's the limit in the virtual world.

Wishing you much virtual success!

Susan Friedmann, CSP, works with organizations that want to grow their target marketing strategies. Susan offers live and virtual programs to increase results and focus on building better relationships with customers, prospects, and advocates in the marketplace.

An exciting, dynamic speaker who delivers top-notch presentations designed to inform, excite, and motivate groups of every size, Susan has also written twelve books, including *Meeting and Event Planning for Dummies, Riches in Niches: How to Make it BIG in a Small Market*, and her latest book, *The Complete Idiot's Guide to Target Marketing*. Visit www.thetradeshowcoach.com or email susan@thetradeshowcoach.com.

Gina Schreck, CSP, is a technology enthusiast, social media expert, and virtual world's evangelist. She is the cofounder and Digital Immigration Officer of Synapse 3Di, a technology and social engagement company, author of several books, including *Getting Geeky with Twitter*, and was the technical editor on the newly released *Complete Idiot's Guide to Social Media*. She hosts weekly events on her virtual world campus in Second Life for folks to come and learn. Visit www.synapse3di.com or email gina@synapse3di.com.

2 5

FOUR BIG REASONS WHY
SPEAKERS SHOULD BLOG

Jeff Korhan

Most people think of blogging as writing. Dig a little deeper, and the interaction and engagement associated with blogging actually make it a digital form of live speaking. There is a presentation, an audience, and most important, a relationship with the audience.

On a theoretical level, writing is speaking and speaking is writing—but it's the human interaction that takes place within the blogging platform that validates the equation in the real world. Emotional connections are made with blog readers just as they are with speaking audiences. While it's not a face-to-face encounter, it is a dialogue—through comments on the blog itself, as well as links and otherwise sharing it on the social Web. These interactions create sustainable nodes on the Web that display a speaker/blogger's expertise. If giving a great speech is the best way for a speaker to get hired again, then a great blog is its digital equivalent, as both serve to communicate on a personal and human level.

Social media is humanizing the Web, replicating human experiences through multimedia interaction. There are many reasons for a professional speaker to blog, but the most relevant are: to showcase expertise; to engage with communities; to develop communication and presentation skills; and to enhance and extend online reputation.

SHOWCASING EXPERTISE

A well-designed blog focuses on solving specific problems for a defined group. In this respect, each blog post validates the writer's expertise—and when augmented with images, audio, and video, it comes to life. Not every speaker is a pure storyteller, but blog stories are practical examples (with a long shelf life!) that help readers see their situations from a new perspective.

Any entrepreneur or small businesses that's serious about marketing needs to be blogging—and speakers are small businesses in the content business. It isn't necessary to have something profound to show the world, just the willingness to be authentic and transparent. A blog is more than a repository of original content, it's a social media hub that influences the other social networks. Unlike the major social networks, however, a blog is 100 percent under the writer's control—and therefore, the ideal way to showcase one's expertise.

ENGAGING WITH THE COMMUNITY

Live presentations are always more successful when there is engagement between the speaker and the audience—even cues as simple as eye contact, facial expressions, and body language. The blogging equivalent is active commenting. While this can take some time to develop, a steady flow of commenting attracts even more interaction. This is why it is essential for bloggers to persevere, even when there are very few readers. Over time, search-engine-indexed material accumulates, with initial readers creating new links to share and circulate the content—eventually creating a vibrant community of fans and influencers.

In contrast, blogging without human interaction is like speaking to an empty room. By skillfully encouraging conversations, the blogger can be more focused and effective while generating a larger following. It starts by making every single visitor feel welcome, followed by reaching out to other bloggers in a similar field with comments on their blogs, in the expectation of reciprocal comments. Search engine optimization and social media optimization can help, but beginning bloggers should focus on the humans and let optimization for the search engines take care of itself. A speaker knows what resonates with audiences; applying that same understanding to Web activities will increase the skill of choosing the key words and phrases for connecting and communicating with that community.

TALENT DEVELOPMENT

When I first started blogging, I chose a weekly video format. My intention was to focus on creating a high-quality presentation that would be consumed much like a live one, and it helped me become more relaxed and authentic in front of the camera.

After a period of time, I elected to use video less frequently so that I could blog on a daily basis. Two things happened. First, I grew a sustainable reader base, which was my primary objective. More important, I developed a spontaneity with my writing that I had not previously known—and I soon realized this skill translated seamlessly to my speaking.

Frequent blogging requires the development of new perspectives. For me, it means I am no longer carrying around a handful of speeches in my mind, but hundreds of stories, practical examples, and anecdotes that have been fully developed, and that naturally find their way into my presentations. This skill has transformed my speaking, liberating my expertise, and guiding me to be a better communicator in all of its forms.

Blogging places practically no limits on a speaker's ability to deliver a message. It's a way to explore and stretch, while practicing audience engagement through the writing, editing, and reworking process. Writing talent and speaking talent go hand in hand.

REPUTATION ENHANCEMENT

There are powerful forces shaping speakers' ability to communicate in the blogosphere. One of those forces is real-time search, which enables search engines to deliver the most current and relevant information for those performing Web searches. Google recently validated this trend, and the fact that blogs are a respected source of relevant content, by introducing a new category search exclusively for blogs. It stands to reason that blogs will increasingly be used to determine whether a speaker is best suited for a particular audience and event.

In fact, I do not maintain a website at present because my blog contains everything about me and necessary to hire me. While I could serve this information up on a website, there would one thing missing—me! Blogging gives a sense of the author's presence as well as the social proof of others being there through the archives of their comments—making the next visitor more likely to hang around. A blog is a home, whereas a website is a place of business—and most people prefer to interact in a social environment.

STEPS FOR SUCCESSFULLY STARTING A BLOG

While the percentage of bloggers is small, it is not for lack of desire. The common refrain of entrepreneurs and small business owners is *I know I should be doing this*. So, what are the top challenges that hold most people back?

1. I don't have enough time.
2. I'm not a very good writer.
3. What should I blog about?
4. How often should I blog?
5. How do I start a blog?

Some solutions will solve multiple challenges simultaneously. For example, posting a short video or an image with a compelling caption addresses the challenges of both time and writing skill. While many concern themselves with how often to blog, consistency is more important than frequency. Nothing turns readers off more quickly than a blog that has apparently been abandoned, either temporarily or permanently.

What to blog about is not only a challenge for new bloggers; it's just as common among long-timers. Everyone is hungry for tips and advice, insights on future trends, and step-by-step methods for getting things done—such as these nine steps for starting a blog:

1. *Define the community.* Do not proceed until you have a clear definition and a mental picture to go with it.
2. *Know why you are blogging.* The actions you want your readers to take will affect the design and content of your blog.
3. *What do you most want to write about?* You have to be passionate about your topic to sustain your blogging efforts.
4. *What is not being done that could be of value?* There are aspects to any topic that are not being addressed, and clues lie within the comments on other blogs in your space.
5. *Choose a descriptive title for your blog.* New readers will read the title of your blog to determine within seconds if they have arrived at the

right place. Use simple language that will resonate with your desired community.

6. *Write a compelling bio that captures your expertise and personality.* This is essential for encouraging new subscribers.

7. *Choose a blog platform that is right for you.* I use and recommend TypePad because they host my blog and provide personal service. Wordpress is another excellent platform for those with a bit of technology savvy.

8. *Start writing.* The only way to find your style is to do the work.

9. *Blog consistently and never stop learning.* You will make your biggest breakthroughs when you persevere and push through every barrier.

Generating speaking leads while developing relationships with influential people serves as its own incentive to keep blogging. That said, the rewards from blogging will happen on their own time. The incubation period can take months and possibly years before you achieve results. Then, unexpectedly, one success will lead to another—a stream of new opportunities.

Blogging can be viewed as marketing and a way to grow business, directly and indirectly. But there are aspects of blogging that transcend normal reasoning. As a human experience of interaction, engagement, and community, blogging has a way of connecting the right speaker with the right clients—and therefore represents an essential practice for speaking success.

Jeff Korhan, MBA, is a new media marketer, an award-winning entrepreneur, and a top-ranked blogger who helps entrepreneurs and small businesses maximize their Web visibility, reputation, and referrals with social media and Internet marketing. Jeff began his career as a Fortune 50 sales and marketing manager. Later, he started and operated a company that was twice named Business of the Year. After 20 successful years he sold his business, and now applies three decades of marketing experience to helping his clients develop sustainable marketing practices that capitalize on emerging small business trends. He is a social media columnist for GIE Media, a frequent guest blogger, and a recognized expert in the green industry, where he has served on several association boards. For more information, visit JeffKorhan.com.

THE INS AND OUTS
OF LICENSING

Jim Hennig, PhD, CSP, CPAE

Normally, a new speaker might be interested in becoming a licensee (someone to whom a license is granted or issued), while experienced speakers would more likely be a licensor (someone who grants permission to use materials). The truth is, however, many veteran speakers use a licensed topic to revisit previous clients with a completely new program; a strategic-thinking novice might begin gathering material with the intention of selling it to other speakers or companies.

In any case, there's money to be made on both sides of the licensing coin, regardless of career duration or primary interest. Here are some simple definitions:

> *Licensee*: One who uses someone else's "stuff" (intellectual property—hereafter referred to as IP) to make a profit and provide enhanced value to a client. This person might alternatively be called:
>
> - a licensee
> - a certified trainer/presenter
> - an associate
> - a regional manager
> - a certified coach
>
> *Licensor*: An individual or company who shares their IP with a licensee so that both make a profit and provide enhanced value to a client. The IP may include a broad base of material, or a

very small item that constitutes a minimal part of a speaker's presentation. Examples include:

- complete presentations with all tools necessary to constitute a topic offering
- small segments of a presentation
- an assessment
- books or workbooks
- DVDs
- coaching programs
- learning tools
- webinars
- e-books

THE EXPRESS LANE TO CONTENT AND CREDIBILITY

The main advantage of becoming a licensee is to increase content and topic offerings quickly. Assuming that the IP is strong and the training provided is effective, there is virtually no way to develop and perfect material as quickly as becoming a licensee. It is the shortest route to presenting solid content to a new or repeat client.

Anyone who has built a body of material for a presentation knows the painstaking time involved. When I began my speaking career, I licensed a content area, was trained quickly on the topic, had many training tools and products available at my disposal, and learned how to effectively market it. It would have taken me 25 to 50 times longer to build a similar program of my own, if that was even possible. In essence, licensing made me an instant expert, generating a reasonable cash flow while I started building my own new topic area. It took an entire year of development before my own materials were ready for the least sophisticated audience.

Some licensors can also be an excellent source of both leads and bookings—though it's important to confirm the booking fees and/or commissions due the licensor.

Finding a licensor can be as simple as ferreting out small parcels of content, an assessment, a training tool, or a role-play that fits well with your program, and then asking for permission. For the licensor, it's easy money, while the licensing program creates instant credibility for the licensee because of the name recognition of the founder, author, or company. Not surprisingly, it's an excellent door opener to meeting planners. And finally, talking shop with fellow licensees can often provide valuable lessons that they have learned.

CAUTION: SPEED COMES AT A COST.

Financial cost is one of the biggest disadvantages of becoming a licensee. In essence, a licensee is paying for the time saved. That can come in the form of an initial licensing or training fee, the continuing royalty or product purchase fee, or the recurrent training or annual renewal fee.

Keep in mind, the costs aren't just monetary: Another disadvantage may be a restrictive non-compete clause. Obviously, licensors must protect their IP with some guidelines in the agreement; the savvy licensee will have an IP attorney review all contractual documents before anything gets a wet signature.

In addition, a licensee has the same program as others have, excepting presentation style or changes permitted by the licensor. This can cause challenges in establishing a distinctive, individual name or brand.

MAGIC FORMULA: CASH FLOW PLUS NAME RECOGNITION.

Creating an immediate cash flow through a licensing or training fee is one of the great advantages of becoming a licensor, followed by the continued royalties or product purchases. With a sufficient number of licensees, consistent cash flow can be maintained over an extended period—even into a comfortable retirement income! Alternatively, the entire company or network of licensees could be sold, resulting in a nice nest-egg lump sum.

Expanding name recognition is another distinct advantage to a licensor. Having licensees throughout the country or world offers exposure to a significantly greater number of people. Without having to travel, the successful licensor might extend his or her material around the globe.

Licensing offers payback for the long and arduous hours of researching, organizing, and perfecting that go into a speaking topic. Indeed, it can actually increase fees as well as the number of engagements. Licensees will often encounter meeting planners who have the budget to afford the higher-visibility originator of a program. (Customarily, a finder's fee is provided to the licensee in this situation.)

Having licensees also affords the opportunity of having a nonnegotiable fee without losing the business. In most cases, licensees will operate at various fee levels; if a potential client cannot afford the licensor's fee, there will most likely be a licensee who fits the budget. (In such cases, the licensee should be contractually obligated to pay a percentage as a finder's fee.)

Finally, the element that many licensors find to be the most gratifying is the satisfaction of helping another speaker succeed in this great business.

CAUTION: LICENSING COMES WITH A COMMITMENT.

For a speaker, one of the most challenging aspects of becoming a licensor is the time necessary to run an effective licensee program. A speaker must ask, "Can I run this and still maintain my primary business of speaking and its necessary cash flow?" Some of the items that will demand time, energy, and attention:

- An effective system for initial and recurrent training. Who will present it? How often? Will training be done individually or as a group? Is recurrent training necessary and, if so, how often?

- A system to maintain quality control of both content and presentation style. If live-session monitoring is not practical, will a video suffice? Can a system of written evaluations by clients be implemented?

- How can you assure the accuracy of royalty reports and payments?

- Who will answer licensees' continued questions as they mature with their businesses?

THE BEST-LAID LICENSOR PLANS . . .

Anyone considering becoming a licensor at some time in the future should start planning now. That includes having discussions with other speakers who are licensing similar topics or items, asking a lot of questions, and keeping notes and files of the best ideas.

Meanwhile, begin formulating the profile of ideal licensees and how they can be found. What qualifiers can be used to assure that they're successful? Licensing

Before Taking the Licensee Leap . . .

Obviously, it's critical to thoroughly investigate any licensing program before becoming involved. Questions should include:

- When did you begin licensing this material? What is your success ratio?

- What causes some of your licensees to be successful and others not?

- May I contact four or five licensees, some who are doing well and others who aren't?

- What could I expect to make if I'm in the top 10 percent of your licensees?

- How can I best see and understand the content of what I am licensing?

- Can you tell me about the training I receive, both initially and later?

- What are the restrictions on me as a licensee?

- Can I have my attorney review the agreement?

fees, annual renewal/training charges, and royalties all need to be determined—taking into consideration what similar licensors are charging.

Then there's the agreement. Will it include non-compete clauses, geographic limitations, or restrictions on the number of licensees in a given area? Again, the details of any agreement need to pass muster with a qualified attorney.

Experimenting with one or two licensees can be a valuable initial step, long before launching a licensing program in earnest. Not only will that help the learning process, but it will generate referrals from successful licensees.

What's the goal in the business of licensing?

> *A properly constructed and successful licensing program*
> *should be a win/win/win, i.e., for licensor/licensee/client.*

Jim Hennig, PhD, CSP, CPAE, is an NSA past president and a 30-year veteran of the speaking business who now licenses his popular Negotiation Training Program to a small number of top speakers and trainers worldwide. In addition, he consults with speakers who want to develop licensing programs and with those seeking to find the ideal license for their interests and speaking style. His popular book, *How to Say It: Negotiating to Win*, was published by Prentice Hall/Penguin in 2008.

ETHICS

ETHICS: THE HOT NEW "E" WORD

Rita Barreto Craig

Palm Beach County, Florida, often conjures images of palm trees, vacations, warm ocean breezes, and sunshine. That would be the "nice" side of this scenic place I have called home for 30 years. However, the adjectives that describe our local government present a less desirable description. *Scandalous, corrupt*, and *unethical* paint a more accurate picture to those who live here.

In the wake of a federal corruption probe, three former county commissioners are now in prison. Two city commissioners recently completed jail sentences. The probes into ethics violations continue, including freebies accepted by contractors, bribes, and under-the-table deals, just to name a few. These violations have resulted in the formation of an independent Ethics Commission.

Ethics. It's the new "E" word. There is now a Palm Beach County Code of Ethics along with a need to spell out its true meaning—and not just for government officials and community leaders. Ethical behavior needs to be interwoven into the very fabric of business and trickle down into our day-to-day dealings with others. For professional speakers, the NSA's Code of Professional Ethics is an essential guide, which reminds us of the importance of two indispensable obligations:

PRESENTING INFORMATION AND IMAGES OF SELF AND BUSINESS THAT ARE TRUE AND CURRENT IN EVERY WAY

According to the Society for Human Resource Management (SHRM), 50 percent of job applicants lie on their employment resumes! And some even get away with it. Of course, there are public speakers and role models who use "creative writing" to highlight their supposed experience on websites and other communications avenues.

We've seen it happen with our public officials, our workplaces, and even in our homes, so we know that sometimes you can temporarily fool people. Consider the employee who was a convicted murderer and went on to work for the school district for three years before being caught. He told the truth on the application, but someone on the inside circumvented the process so that he was hired despite the prohibition within the state of Florida.

Our reputations must be guarded. When in doubt, we must err on the conservative side. In recent years, we have been inundated with examples of ethics violations in the business world. Enron, WorldCom, and Adelphia are just a few. Some entire professions are the butt of late-night talk show jokes, and the mere mention of ethics within the same sentence is nothing short of laughable. Professional speakers can become similarly derailed, unless they choose to model the highest level of the NSA's ethical competency.

As speakers, we are not required to focus on ethics as much as those employed by publicly traded companies, who must have ethics codes and training. Yet we can and should learn from others who have thrown their excellent reputations into the gutter. It makes good business sense to do the right thing, whether or not you are required to by legislation.

This poses a good question. When faced with an opportunity to make a huge profit while compromising honesty, does honesty always win? If so, customer loyalty is built, revenues increase, and employees feel proud to be a part of an organization they know will always treat them well. The bottom line is that demonstrating uncompromised ethics builds your bottom line and brand.

Several years ago, my parents gave our son a plaque that reads, "Character is doing what's right when nobody is looking," a quote from U.S. Congressman J. C. Watts. We are presented with choices every day. So, should we always stick to doing what's right, or should we embellish our qualifications—whether personal or business—to fit the need? These ethical challenges are probably more prevalent today because of a down economy, causing speakers and others to do things they would never have thought of before. A slow economy shouldn't mean sacrificing values. Most people understand they should behave ethically, but as NSA speakers, how can we ensure that we adhere to ethical behaviors?

Define Your Values

Some businesses and individuals define their core values and beliefs in statements about how they will conduct their business and how they will treat others. Such statements define what is important and don't typically change.

One way to approach the development of values is to brainstorm words that define what is important to you. Consider attributes like honesty, trust, creativity, fun, excellence, and collaboration. Write a present-tense statement about each value and do so with strong thought, emphasis, and conviction. Be sure not to put more than one value in each sentence. Look at the two examples listed below:

> I will *try to* demonstrate honesty in all my interactions. *(Would you hire this person?)*
>
> I demonstrate honesty in all my interactions. *(You are hired!)*

The goal is to continue focusing on model behaviors. When there is a misstep in values, the important thing is to be honest and admit failure, correct the situation, and learn from it. In the customer service arena, this is called a "service recovery."

After you come up with five or six values, honestly assess whether these are *your* true values or just something that will look good as a selling feature. Values should come from your heart and be adhered to at all times.

Additionally, values should be readdressed periodically. If you fall off track, identify examples of when you did or did not model appropriate behavior(s). Then implement an action plan to ensure future success. Get feedback from colleagues if you wish. Ask them how they would describe your values. Are you in sync, or have you been wearing blinders in certain circumstances? Whichever the case may be, make sure your values are in front of you every day. Use them for more effective decision-making and to help build your winning brand.

WORKING ETHICALLY AND COLLABORATIVELY WITH INDIVIDUALS AND GROUPS WITH WHOM SPEAKERS OFTEN INTERACT

Many organizations today are forming partnerships and working regionally to capitalize on relationships and resources. As with any relationship, it is important to have a thorough understanding of a business partner's values. How many speakers take the time to discuss their values with individuals and/or groups?

Several years ago, many banks merged, only to experience high turnover of executives within the first year, often because of the disconnection of values. One bank may have had a strong commitment to its community, while the new one did not. Therefore, the leaders found themselves working for an organization that did not share their values and work became just that: work. The passion was gone. When working with a client, you should share your values with each another up front so that each party can assess whether it will be a beneficial relationship.

Here are 10 additional guidelines for ethical speaking:

1. **Be qualified to speak**. Everyone can be book smart (or online savvy). However, a really great speaker knows what he or she is talking about, and it shows. So, whenever you are presented with an opportunity to deliver in front of a group you have been dying to work with, make sure you can deliver.

2. **Be prepared**. Allow ample time to conduct research, alter your presentation (if needed), and develop a customized plan that is a perfect 10. Nothing short of outstanding belongs on your list of services. Delivering anything less can easily damage your brand. The audience can tell if you have done your homework, or if you are delivering a speech that is on remote control. If you want to engage the audience, prepare with an exceptional presentation—just for them!

3. **Know your audience and presentation logistics**. Every audience is unique. That's one of the many elements that make this business fun! Take the time to discuss who will be in the room, terms to eliminate, and terms to highlight. Knowing as much as possible about the audience ahead of time will build comfort. If you have the luxury of meeting participants before the presentation, it will jumpstart your connection with them. Develop a checklist to use when speaking to a potential client. Include questions regarding the reason for the presentation, overall objectives (i.e., What do you want the crowd to leave with?), audience information, hot points, key competitors, etc.

4. **Give appropriate credit.** If asked if you have ever spoken to a similar au-

dience, tell the truth. Also, give credit where credit is due. No one likes listening to a speaker share a "personal story" when they can recall hearing that same story during their favorite movie. Or listening to a speaker who takes credit for someone else's ideas. The Internet is a wealth of information. Make sure you always cite sources. As speakers, we cannot falsify or misrepresent data. As a facilitator, make sure you aren't using pirated software, music, or images. That behavior is a clear ethics violation and can cost you your credibility.

5. **Don't bait and switch.** The title of your presentation and objectives need to match what you're delivering. Attendees can get pulled into workshops with zippy titles and action-oriented objectives. Sometimes it's a major home run and time well spent. Other times it's a major disappointment to learn that the presentation is completely different from what was marketed. Once your speech and title are written, go back and read it objectively to make sure the title reflects what the speech is about. Deliver what you promise.

6. **Speak with facts.** Always present an honest picture of the situation. Some speakers only present one side of the story with certainty and conviction—even though they are aware that other options exist. It might make the information learned much more interesting and profound to leave the audience with something they'll remember. However, altering the facts is strictly unethical. After you have prepared a presentation, go back and make sure it is accurate and balanced. Your presentation will be enhanced if you add facts, statistics, and sources relevant to your presentation.

7. **Focus on the topic, rather than self-promotion.** Chances are the audience came to hear about the topic that was promoted, not you. Although having a captive audience at your disposal poses an opportunity to sell items, don't ever lose sight of the meat of your main topic.

8. **Words and actions should be harmonious.** Never use inappropriate comments, jokes, photos, or music during a presentation. Remember, your reputation is all you have. Although you may currently have a stellar reputation, it can all be erased in a second by violating the Golden Rule. As an example, I was once hired to deliver a speech to a Fortune

500 company. Upon my arrival, my key contact shared his frustration with his VP for telling a sexist joke earlier in the day. He said he looked around the room and could see the appalled audience all but crawling under their seats.

9. **Confidentiality.** When working with clients, we sometimes gain inside information about the culture of the organization and/or the audience. Some companies even require a confidentiality agreement. We must be vigilant about protecting confidential communication and information.

10. **Mentoring.** When NSA was originally founded by Cavett Robert, CSP, CPAE, he strongly believed that information should be shared so that all could learn from one another's experiences. Hence, we should always have each other's best interests at heart by providing open and honest feedback. This includes consistently sharing factual information and acting with sincerity.

Never forget the importance of ethics on a personal and professional level. In the words of Martin Luther King,

> Cowardice asks the question; 'Is it safe?' Expediency asks the question; 'Is it politic?' Vanity asks the question; 'Is it popular?' But conscience asks the question, 'Is it right?' And there comes a time when one must take a position that is neither safe, nor politic, nor popular . . . but because conscience tells one it is right.

Rita Barreto Craig is president and founder of Top Tier Leadership, a human resources consulting firm located in Palm Beach Gardens, Florida. Formerly the Craig Group, Top Tier is committed to providing clients around the globe with innovative solutions to meet their business needs. Her diverse background includes extensive management experience and specialized professional work in a variety of areas, including strategic planning, employee relations, antiharassment training, diversity, coaching, leadership, work/life balance, and facilitation. A dynamic and accomplished speaker, trainer, and coach, Rita has presented throughout the world. Visit www.thecraig-group.net.

WALK YOUR OWN TALK

Al Walker, CSP, CPAE

As professional speakers, as in any industry, people count on us to do what we say we are going to do and when; to be who we say we are; to treat others with mutual respect; and to never use material that others created and worked diligently to develop and then try to pass it off as our own. At best, it would be a source of embarrassment; at worst, it could result in an appearance in a court of law for infringing on intellectual property—and either way, guaranteeing infamy within the meetings and speaking industry. Dr. Henry Kissinger once said, "You can spend a lifetime building your integrity and tear it all down in a moment." He was right.

The ethics statement every National Speakers Association member must sign states very clearly that we are to play by the rules of good conduct. If we don't, we can be reprimanded and even kicked out of the association. These are not just empty words— they have teeth.

Several years ago, an NSA member was given one of our highest honors, and shortly after, it was discovered this person was misusing the title of Ph.D. in promotional materials. Robert Henry, CSP, CPAE, an NSA past president and Cavett Award Winner, beloved friend and partner in Platform Professionals— and a stickler for academic authenticity—did a little investigative work and discovered that this individual did not have a Ph.D.

When confronted, this person claimed to have completed the class work, but not the dissertation—saying that ABD (All But Dissertation) was the same as having a doctorate. Robert responded, "No, ABD is the same as YAGAD–'You Ain't Got a Doctorate.'" It's akin to a person who, having been invited to a party, had gotten to the front door, decided not to go in, and later told people he or she had been there.

When asked to remove any mention of a doctorate from promotional materials, this speaker refused to do so. As a result, this individual was stripped of honors and expelled from NSA. After subsequently repenting and agreeing to remove all references to a doctorate, the person's membership and honors were reinstated. Alas, within a matter of months, PhD mentions began reappearing. The NSA Ethics committee once again stripped the honors and expelled the individual from membership, this time with the assurance that it was permanent.

When speakers tout an unearned degree or a mail order "read five books, do a book report, and we'll give you a doctorate" degree, they are attempting to gain false credibility. They are willing to risk losing all credibility if the discrepancy is discovered, in hopes that their false credentials will gain them credibility in the marketplace before it happens. They know they are not being truthful or have taken some meaningless shortcut to "degreedom"—yet, like so many lies, the more they tell themselves and others they have a degree and get away with it, the more they actually begin to believe the lies and the more they will vigorously defend them.

There are other examples of fraudulent behavior that have cost people their membership in NSA; there are some, however, who may do more damage in the long run than those who blatantly misbehave. These are the folks who live on the edge of integrity, and even though it may take longer, that, too, will eventually catch up with them.

Several years ago, I was talking to a meeting planner who was considering not hiring any more professional speakers, because of an experience the previous year. Pressed for details, the meeting planner proceeded to share with me in great detail how rude, demanding, disrespectful, and mean-spirited the speaker had been. This wasn't the personality their organization had seen on the speaker's demo video, and the differences between the off-stage and on-stage persona were stark.

At this point, I asked, "What else did (and I gave her a professional speaker's name) do?"

There was a long pause and she said, "I didn't tell you who it was, but that *is* who I was talking about." The name had been easy to guess, because she had described a person whose poor reputation was notorious within NSA. Now, before you accuse me of an ethics violation for saying something bad about a fellow member of NSA, I didn't say anything bad about that person, she did—I just confirmed who it was.

Long-time NSA member, and a partner of mine in Platform Professionals, Doc Blakley has told the story several times of how, years ago, he was speaking to a group and the further he got into his talk, the more uncomfortable he became and the more uncomfortable he felt the audience becoming. When he finished, instead of hearing the usual roaring round of applause, he received only a smattering of weak, polite clapping.

Doc later found out the issue: He had delivered the same speech as the group had heard at the previous year's gathering. Doc was stunned. Here is a man who is the epitome of integrity. He has earned his CSP and CPAE, and he is a Cavett Award Winner. He earned a doctorate in Animal Husbandry from Sam Houston State University in Huntsville, Texas. He is revered and highly respected in his hometown of Wharton, Texas. Yet, in this situation, his integrity was questioned because someone decided to memorize his speech and pass it off as his own. Even though he did nothing wrong, Doc was unable to repair his relationship with the meeting planner. And, I should add, the meeting planner would not tell me or Doc who the previous speaker had been. (Trust me, we've tried to find out and it remains an unsolved mystery.)

It is with the two subjects' permission that I share this next story about how one of my closest friendships with a speaker started off on shaky ground more than 25 years ago. A friend of mine who teaches at a local school had just heard a speaker who shared a hilarious story about a beauty pageant contestant whose talent misfired.

I recognized it instantly as a Jeanne Robertson, CSP, CPAE, signature story—indeed, anyone who has been in the speaking business for more than five minutes knows that is one of her most popular tales. I gave Jeanne a call, but she did not overreact—her approach was that it was surely a mistake, and she let it ride. Shortly after that, however, Jeanne's former roommate at Auburn University heard this same speaker repeat Jeanne's story. She immediately called Jeanne, who then decided it was time to take action.

Rather than coming across as the "material police," however, Jeanne decided to approach the new speaker as a friend, and the new speaker responded in kind. Jeanne explained that if she were to speak to that same group at a later date, or if someone in the new speaker's audience heard Jeanne somewhere else later on, they'd wonder not only if the story was true, but to whom it actually belonged. The new speaker had not realized that, even though she gave Jeanne credit for the story, there was potential for damage to both Jeanne and the new speaker. As it happens, the new speaker handled it perfectly also. New to the business, she didn't know that she shouldn't use other people's stories, regardless of whether she gave them credit. She quickly apologized and immediately stopped using the anecdote, which is what any honest person would do.

Here, as Paul Harvey would say, is "the rest of the story." This new speaker, Jane Jenkins Herlong, CSP, participated in the first timer's event at the NSA annual convention in Orlando, Florida, a few months later. She asked Jeanne to attend and, in front of their peers and several hundred attendees, explained what had happened and the problems associated with using others' material, and she used it as a learning opportunity for speakers who are new to the trade.

If there has ever been a wonderful example of all's well that end's well, this is it. The lesson is clear: Ethical professional speakers create and use their own material, and wouldn't think of trying to capitalize on the material of any other speaker. Jeanne and Jane are classy women, the two remain best of friends, and I am proud to call them my friends, too.

In one of my books, *The Sheep Thief*, I included, with permission, a list of statements titled "The Paradoxical Commandments." It is a piece written by Dr. Kent M. Keith when he was a 19-year-old student at Harvard as part of a student handbook titled *The Silent Revolution: Dynamic Leadership in the Student Council*. A more widely known version of the list of statements is a poem titled "Do It Anyway," a rewritten version of Dr. Keith's piece credited to Mother Teresa.

The following is taken from Dr. Keith's commandments:

People are illogical, unreasonable, and self-centered.

Love them anyway.

And now, for comparison, a similar line from Mother Teresa's version:

People are often unreasonable, irrational, and self-centered.

Forgive them anyway.

Now before anyone jumps down my throat for impugning the integrity of Mother Teresa, please know that is not what I am doing. Her website and others give Dr. Kent credit for his orignal work. My point is meant to illustrate that in today's business world, everything is under so much scrutiny that even the least little hint of impropricty can become an integrity issue.

It is incumbent upon all of us to do as Mike Huckabee, former presidential candidate, an ordained minister, and now host of his own TV show, extols in the title of one of his latest books: *Do the Right Thing*. Isn't that what a person of integrity always strives to do: the right thing?

A Lesson About Intellectual Property

A chapter on ethics would be incomplete without a discussion on intellectual property (IP), which refers to creations of the mind that have commercial value. For speakers, IP could be keynotes, speeches, signature stories, books, articles and recordings, to name a few.

IP is an asset, just like real estate, a car, jewelry, furniture, etc., and needs to be protected from plagiarism and copyright infringement.

In the world of professional speaking, plagiarism is falsely representing another speaker's material (speeches, stories, phrases, opinions, etc.) as your own original work. It involves deception and is dishonest and unethical. Plagiarism is not the same as copyright infringement, which is a violation of the rights of a copyright holder when material protected by copyright is used without consent. If plagiarism involves copyright infringement, it is illegal.

There are two ways to protect intellectual property: trademarks and copyrights.

A trademark protects a product identifier, such as the name, logo, and visual attributes (color, design, etc.), that distinguishes it from other products or services. Trademarks can be renewed forever as long as they are being used in business. Federal trademark registration provides the strongest protection, but each state also has its own trademark protection.

A copyright protects works of authorship, such as books, music, and works of art that have been tangibly expressed. The Library of Congress registers copyrights that last the life of the author plus 70 years. Copyright registration requires filing a simple form, paying a modest fee, and submitting a copy of the work you want to protect.

Consult an attorney who is familiar with the categories of IP to determine if your work can and should be trademarked or copyrighted.

Al Walker, CSP, CPAE, is an internationally recognized speaker, author, leader, trainer, and businessman. He is past president of the National Speakers Association, a Cavett Award Winner, a Master of Influence Award Winner, and a member of the CPAE Speaker Hall of Fame. Using his motivational, inspirational, humorous style, Al speaks on and teaches leadership, customer service, creative thinking, teamwork, professionalism, and personal growth. He is the author of *Thinking Big & Living Large* (Almar Publishing) and *The Sheep Thief* (Tremendous Life Books). Al can be reached at al@alwalker.com or through www.alwalker.com

SETTING A CODE OF PROFESSIONAL ETHICS FOR THE SPEAKING PROFESSION

Stacy Tetschner, CAE

Professional ethics are written and unwritten principles and values that govern the decisions and actions of participants within a profession. In the business world, every profession upholds standards for determining the difference between good and bad decision making and behavior in the profession, as a whole.

A Code of Professional Ethics establishes and maintains the standards, reputation, and public confidence in the speaking profession. All speakers must adhere to a personal code of ethics at a minimum and hopefully to the standard set within the profession overall to provide those that hire them with the confidence that they will deliver the services they have agreed to and that the material they are presenting is theirs and not taken from someone else.

In order to be a member of the National Speakers Association, a speaker must agree to subscribe to the NSA Code of Professional Ethics as a condition of membership. The intent is that each member will strive to uphold the values, reputation, and legacy of NSA as the largest professional association that represents speakers and sets the ethical standard for the profession. Fellow members can then trust that their colleagues within NSA operate at this minimum foundation of business practice and those hiring NSA speakers rest assured that they are engaging professionals who operate their business at a high level.

Following is the Code of Professional Ethics that NSA members must adhere to:

Article 1—Representation: The NSA member has an obligation to him- or herself and to NSA to represent him- or herself truthfully, professionally, and in a non-misleading manner. The NSA member shall be honest and accurate in presenting qualifications and experience in the member's communication with others.

Article 2—Professionalism: The NSA member shall act, operate his/her business, and speak in a most professional and ethical manner so as neither to offend nor bring discredit to him- or herself, the speaking profession, or his or her fellow NSA members.

Article 3—Research: The NSA member shall exert efforts to understand each client's organization, approaches, goals and culture in advance of a presentation, in order to professionally apply his or her expertise to meet each client's needs.

Article 4—Intellectual Property: The NSA member shall avoid using—either orally or in writing—materials, titles, or thematic creations originated by others unless approved in writing by the originator.

Article 5—Respect & Collegiality: The NSA member shall maintain a collegial relationship with fellow members that is based on respect, professional courtesy, dignity, and the highest ethical standards.

Article 6—Confidentiality: The NSA member shall maintain and respect the confidentiality of business or personal affairs of clients, agents, and other speakers.

Article 7—Business Practices: The NSA member is obligated to maintain a high level of ethical standards and practices in order to assist in protecting the public against fraud or any unfair practice in the speaking profession and shall attempt to eliminate from the profession all practices that could bring discredit to the speaking profession.

Article 8—Diversity: The NSA member shall not participate in any agreement or activity that would limit or deny access to the marketplace to any other speaker, to a client, or to the public. This includes, but not limited to, economic factors, race, ethnicity, creed, color, sex, age, sexual orientation, disability, religion, or country of national origin of any party.

Stacy Tetschner, CAE, has been the CEO of the National Speakers Association (NSA) since 1998 and has served in a variety of management capacities for the organization since 1991. He has worked closely with NSA's Ethics Committee to continually update, maintain, and enforce the NSA Code of Professional Ethics, which serves as the ethical standard for the entire speaking profession. You can contact him for this or any matters related to NSA at (480) 968-2552 or via e-mail at stacy@nsaspeaker.org.

WHY SHOULD YOU JOIN A PROFESSIONAL ASSOCIATION?

Membership in a professional association is an investment in your professional credibility, your career development, and your personal growth. It is a clear indicator of your serious commitment to your profession.

People join professional associations to reap membership benefits. Associations publish magazines, journals, and newsletters bursting with up-to-date information to keep members current on issues and developments in their profession. They hold conventions, conferences, seminars, labs, workshops, and other educational events where professionals can acquire new knowledge or hone their skills. In fact, many professional associations develop professional educational programs and perform professional certification to confirm that a member is proficient in his or her subject area.

Membership in an association is an excellent way to meet, network, and stay connected to other professionals in your field who are going somewhere and want to share their knowledge and experiences along their journey. Membership also enables you to build your network of professionals in the field.

These are sound reasons for joining a professional association, but what's the main reason to become a member?

Membership can help you succeed.

THE SPEAKING PROFESSION

Throughout history, great speakers have touched millions of lives worldwide, and have inspired and motivated people to become leaders, achieve financial prosperity, improve their relationships, and lead healthier lives. Today's speaking profession is composed of keynote speakers, motivational speakers, coaches, trainers, facilitators, consultants, and others who deliver their message and impart knowledge to live or virtual audiences.

Professional speaking can be a very lucrative career, or a complementary tool for promoting products and services. Speakers can enjoy fun, freedom, and financial prosperity while they share their valuable motivational messages to audiences across the United States and across the globe.

Regardless of the industry or discipline in which your expertise as a speaker falls, people who speak professionally have many things in common. Many are entrepreneurs or small business owners who share the same challenges related to products and services, keeping up with technological advances, and anticipating trends.

Speaking also can be a lonely profession, with long hours, hectic travel schedules, and an ever-changing cast of characters (clients). By joining a professional association, speakers can expand their network and connect with others who can relate to their experiences on the platform and on the road.

The National Speakers Association (NSA), the leading organization for speakers and those who aspire to a speaking career, brings these individuals together to address the gamut of issues in a caring and sharing community.

MAKE A BIGGER PIE

In 1972, Cavett Robert, CSP, CPAE, envisioned a forum where speakers could convene to improve their presentation skills, increase their business, and exchange ideas and share experiences with their peers. He felt that everyone involved in the speaking profession would benefit from growing the number and quality of professional speakers, which he referred to as "making a bigger pie." Robert founded the National Speakers Association the following year, and its membership grew rapidly. By 1980, there were 1,000 members, resulting from very little promotion or solicitation, mostly from speakers telling other speakers.

Robert displayed an uncanny ability for inspiring others and sharing his wisdom and expertise. "A desire to help others is our most noble attribute; it gives immortal momentum to life and is our only certain path to heaven," Robert said.

Today, NSA is a community of thousands of speaking professionals all over the world—a community where the pursuit of knowledge and the sharing of ideas is a way of life. Membership includes experts in a variety of industries and disciplines, who reach audiences as trainers, educators, humorists, motivators, consultants, authors, and more. Since 1973, NSA has provided resources and education to advance the skills, integrity, and value of its members and the speaking profession.

NSA works hard to enable speakers to achieve their business goals. By constantly taking the pulse of the marketplace, NSA offers valuable education, tools, resources, and support to help speakers meet professional challenges in the face of economic conditions, and opportunities to develop their skills so they can create the speaking businesses of their dreams.

NSA members help other speakers sharpen their platform skills, make their businesses run more efficiently, and show speakers how to use the latest marketing techniques to cast a wider net for attracting more business and building a larger client base.

This dynamic combination of education and networking opportunities provides literally hundreds of income-producing ideas for professional speakers.

IT'S ALL ABOUT MEETINGS

By attending NSA events, including chapter meetings, conferences, labs, and the annual convention, members learn how other speakers have created multiple streams of income. They can use this information to increase their speaking businesses to new levels of profitability.

Who goes to NSA meetings? Professional speakers, trainers, consultants, aspiring speakers, and meeting industry professionals, such as bureau owners, meeting planners, and association executives—anyone who wants to enter the world of professional speaking. Certain meetings also have special programming for speaker's staff, partners, and youth.

From the intimate setting of an NSA conference to the electricity of an NSA annual convention, members and non-members alike return year after year to see old friends, gain inspiration, and obtain valuable education, along with hundreds of "aha!" moments, and cull ideas they can use to build their speaking businesses. During the year, speakers can stay in regular contact using social media, for example, by joining NSA's various Facebook groups.

NSA CHAPTERS

Chapters are the heart of NSA, where speakers can unite at the local level for networking, education, and camaraderie. Each of NSA's 39 chapters has its own personality and offers a variety of programming, such as speakers' schools, mentor programs, showcase presentations, and educational meetings. Attendance at chapter meetings is exceptionally high, even when members must travel three hours each way to attend a meeting.

PROFESSIONAL EXPERT GROUPS

There are thirteen "Professional Expert Groups" (PEGs) that focus on a unique skill, topic area, or market. PEGS attract like-minded individuals with varying levels of experience in the following areas: Business Coaching, Consulting, Diversity, e-PEG, Educators, Facilitators, Health and Wellness, Humor, Motivational/ Keynote Speakers, Sales Experts, Seminar/Workshop Leaders, Storytellers, and Writers/Publishers.

PEGs provide a venue where speakers can connect and collaborate for a nominal fee. By joining a PEG, speakers can listen in to periodic teleseminars to develop their skills, learn the secrets of success from masters in their area of focus, gain access to other PEG members to brainstorm ideas, and attend closed-door PEG sessions at conferences and conventions.

GLOBAL SPEAKERS FEDERATION

NSA members have access to the tools and resources offered by the Global Speakers Federation (GSF), which is composed of speaking organizations in nine major international markets. GSF provides opportunities for speakers to expand their message by connecting them with colleagues all over the world who can help them enter global markets with greater ease. For more information, visit www.globalspeakers.net.

MEMBER BENEFITS PROVIDE ONGOING EDUCATION

NSA University

NSA University, founded in 2010, is dubbed "The Ultimate Online Source for

Speaker Education." NSA-U is an online education destination for obtaining digital recordings from conferences, conventions, meetings, and other content-rich programs. NSA-U also leverages the power of high technology to offer its well-attended Webinar series, with expert presenters delivering relevant new content every month.

When you want some education on demand, NSA-U is a time-saving and cost-effective alternative for busy speakers who want to hone their presentation skills and increase their knowledge of the speaking profession—right in the comfort of their office or home.

Speaker Magazine

Speaker magazine, NSA's official award-winning publication, is published 10 times annually in print and digital formats. Speaker provides members and non-members with the latest marketing and branding strategies, legislative updates, tips on running a speaking business more efficiently, and innovative ideas from top professionals worldwide. Articles are contributed by working speakers, who generously share their knowledge from the trenches of their speaking businesses.

NSA Now

NSA Now is a quarterly newsletter that features timely information about membership benefits, welcomes new members, and provides interesting news bytes relevant to professional speakers. *NSA Now* accompanies the January/February, April, July/August, and October issues of *Speaker* magazine.

Voices of Experience Audio Magazine

Voices of Experience is an audio magazine in which top achievers share their experiences to bring members vital, up-to-date information on every facet of the speaking profession. Members receive VOE CD 10 times each year, mailed with each issue of *Speaker* magazine. The latest editions are also available on podcast.

Earn Professional Certification

The Certified Speaking Professional (CSP) designation, conferred by the

National Speakers Association and the Global Speakers Federation (GSF), is the speaking profession's international measure of professional platform skill. Professional speakers who have earned the CSP designation bring a proven track record of experience and expertise to meetings.

The CSP designation is earned through a rigorous five-year certification process in which a speaker must demonstrate competence in a combination of standards in platform skills, business management, education, and association. Only 10 percent of professional speakers have earned this elite status.

Awards and Recognition

NSA recognizes the men and women who have made a difference in the lives of their audiences and other professional speakers. Cavett Robert, CSP, CPAE, was known to say, "It's amazing how much people can do when they divorce themselves from concern over who gets the credit."

From guiding and inspiring other members to defining excellence on the platform, from exemplifying ethical behavior to selflessly devoting time to make NSA the great organization it is, some members and non-members stand out as extraordinary and are recognized and honored with the following:

- The Cavett Award
- CPAE Speaker Hall of Fame
- President's Award for Distinguished Service
- Lifetime Membership
- Master of Influence Award
- Philanthropist of the Year Award

THE NSA FOUNDATION: SERVING, SHARING, SUPPORTING

The NSA Foundation is the charitable arm of NSA, and serves members and the public through:

- Financial help for NSA members and their families who are facing health crises or are victims of natural disaster emergencies.
- Grants to NSA members who need help with their dues or meeting registration fees.

- Scholarships for full-time junior, senior or graduate students attending an accredited college or university, who have a burning desire to become professional speakers.
- Funding for research related to the speaking profession.
- Grants to help charitable organizations communicate through technology.

Contributions come from three basic sources:

1. Major gifts donated to establish various funds .
2. Memorial and other contributions from individual NSA members and chapters.
3. Fundraising events such as seminars, receptions and parties at NSA conventions and workshops.

Thanks to the generous contributions of NSA speakers, many worthy individuals have received financial support when they needed it most.

Do you want to succeed in your speaking business? You owe it to yourself to learn more about the benefits of NSA membership by calling (480) 968-2552 or visiting www.NSASpeaker.org.